The Ultimate Awareness, an Eternal Constant

Volume One

Writings by the Author

The Ultimate
Prayers and Excerpts from The Word
Success Is Normal, Just Be Yourself,
   Your Eternal Identity
Fulfillment of Purpose, Volume One
Fulfillment of Purpose, Volume Two
You Are the Splendor
Gems & Poems of The Ultimate
The Gospel According to Thomas
Three Essential Steps
The Omnipresent I AM, Volume One
The Omnipresent I AM, Evidenced, Volume Two
The Ultimate Awareness, an Eternal Constant,
   Volume One
The Ultimate Awareness, an Eternal Constant,
   Volume Two

These and other books available through:
Mystics of the World
Eliot, Maine
www.mysticsoftheworld.com

The Ultimate Awareness, an Eternal Constant

Volume One

Marie S. Watts

The Ultimate Awareness, an Eternal Constant
Volume One
by Marie S. Watts

Mystics of the World First Edition 2016   }9 6 9
Published by Mystics of the World
ISBN-13: 978-0692667569
ISBN -10: 0692667563

For information contact:
Mystics of the World
Eliot, Maine
www.mysticsoftheworld.com

Photography by © Dr. Joel Murphy 2016
www.DrJMphotography.zenfolio.com
Printed by CreateSpace
Available from Mystics of the World and Amazon.com

Contents

Foreword

There is but one Absolute Truth, namely, *God is All—All is God*. Within the pages of this book, you will find this basic Truth stated over and over again. There are a variety of words in which this Absolute Truth may be revealed and presented, but the basic premise must ever remain the same and inviolate. Within the writings of the Ultimate you will find no violation of—and no departure from—this Absolute Truth.

This first volume of classnotes presents the revelations we experienced during the first half of the 1968 class given in Vista, California. Those who attended are aware of the glorious illumination experienced during the sessions, and many have reported further revelation and illumination since the class. A few words of explanation may be helpful to those who did not attend the class.

Our classes in Vista consisted of morning and evening sessions. The five morning sessions were one complete class, and the five evening sessions were one complete class, with both comprising one *continuous* class. As stated before, this volume presents the first half of the classwork, and the second volume of this work is a presentation of the second half; thus, it is of the utmost importance that this first volume be read, studied, and contemplated before reading the second volume of these classnotes. Actually, the Absolute Truth presented in this volume is a most necessary preparation for the revelations of the second volume.

Those of you who are veterans in the study of the Ultimate know full well that all revelation is Self-revelation. And you realize that this Truth is not being revealed *to* you. Therefore, you will simply read and contemplate the contents herein as full open Consciousness. In short, you will know that the Consciousness that reveals the Absolute Truth is the Consciousness that reads and contemplates this Truth. The revelator and the revelation are one and the same — *and you are that One.*

Those of you who are not familiar with the writings of the Ultimate may, just at first, find the terminology somewhat puzzling. Some of you have said that we learn to speak and write in an entirely new vocabulary, and this is quite true. You see, we can only speak and write as the words are revealed. However, you will realize that you *are* the Consciousness that does clearly perceive every Absolute Truth you are reading. You will not make *any* effort to understand the words or the statements. Rather, you will joyously, freely, and effortlessly read and *let* this Truth reveal Itself as the Consciousness that *you are.*

Those of you who are familiar with these writings will find some reiteration of basic Truths that have been stated previously. But you will bear with us, knowing that we are only replacing the building blocks for a far more wondrous and glorious revelatory structure. The same basic Truth must always be the foundation, but the revelations of this Truth are constant, and they are ever more beautiful and complete.

The Absolute Truths presented in these two volumes are being revealed as the fulfillment of a glorious purpose. And the same Presence that reveals these Truths is the Presence that fulfills the purpose of the revelations. As you read, study, and contemplate the Truths herein revealed, you will find this fulfillment of God's purpose being experienced as *your* Life, *your* Consciousness, and *your* Body. You will perceive that your Life is the Life that you *are*; your Consciousness is the Consciousness that you *are*; and your Body is the Body that you *are*. Truly, *God is All—All is God*.

Boundless Light and Love,
Marie S. Watts

Chapter I

Basic Premise of the Ultimate Absolute

This is a book that is based firmly and totally on the one basic Truth—*God is All—All is God*. This is an Absolute Truth, and we do not deviate from this completely Absolute Truth by one iota.

Those who have thoroughly studied this entire Absolute approach that we call *The Ultimate* will clearly perceive and understand every Absolute Truth that is herein presented. (Actually, all Truth is Absolute Truth because anything that is true—or Truth—is absolutely, wholly, and entirely true, or an eternal, constant Fact.) Nonetheless, it is to be hoped that you are familiar with these writings. However, if some of the statements in this book appear to be somewhat obscure, you may rest assured that before you have finished reading the final chapter you will understand, perceive, and realize that you actually *are* every Truth that you have read within these pages.

The first necessity in reading this book is a full open Consciousness. If, just at first, some of the statements should appear unreasonable, illogical, or perhaps even ridiculous, don't be at all surprised or perturbed. Just shrug them off for the moment and continue reading. It is not wisdom to attempt to interpret that which you read as you go along. That which is called a thinking mind attempts to interpret. This book will reveal its own Absolute Truths in, through, and as your own Consciousness. Do you ask why this is true? The answer is that every Absolute Truth you can ever read, hear, or perceive is already present as the very Consciousness that *you* are. Actually, you are reading the Truth *that you are*.

Jesus knew this when he stated, "I am the truth …" (John 14:6). Well, beloved One, you also are the Truth. So the contents of this book are no stranger to you; you will ultimately recognize them as being your own Consciousness.

The word *Consciousness* is an exceedingly important word in our Ultimate vocabulary. There are several words that are also of tremendous importance to our perception of this Absolute Truth. But we will discuss these words as we encounter them. Right now, let us explore this word *Consciousness*. To many, it appears that when we refer to Consciousness we are speaking of the so-called human — or born — consciousness that seems to be conscious of and as "man with breath in his nostrils" and all his apparent problems. Nothing could be further from the truth. To us, this word *Consciousness* is always capitalized. It denotes God. *Consciousness is God*.

Again and again, we have said that God is all Substance. We have also spoken and read about spiritual Substance, or of Spirit as being Substance.

Well, Spirit and Consciousness are one and the same Substance. This word *Spirit* means much to many students of the Truth, but to us, the word *Consciousness* has a very special meaning. This is true because Consciousness is awareness. It is our very awareness that we exist. In other words, it is our awareness of being. And as you can see, it is important to realize that our awareness of being is truly the Substance that we are. As you continue on perusing this book, you will increasingly realize the importance of perceiving that Consciousness—our very awareness that we exist—really is our only Substance.

There are four words that are paramount in our perception of the Absolute Truth. These words, when capitalized, signify, or symbolize, the All, the Totality, which is God. They are *Consciousness, Life, Mind* (Intelligence), and *Love*. We do not deal with that which is called a human or mortal consciousness, human mind, human life, or human love.

Consciousness is the boundless, infinite, omnipresent, constant awareness of being, which is God aware of being that God *is*, all that God is, and *only* that which God is. Life is the eternal, uninterrupted, living Substance in action, which is Consciousness alive. Mind is the indivisible, living, conscious Intelligence, which constantly governs Its Allness—Infinitude—in and as perfect, orderly, intelligent activity. And Love, the greatest of all symbols, is the inseparable Oneness of everyone and everything that comprises this boundless Universe.

Furthermore, Love is complete Harmony and eternal, constant Perfection. All Love is *perfect* Love. We will have much more to say about the foregoing four words as we continue. You will find that they are of tremendous importance in your spiritual vocabulary.

Now that you have read thus far in this book, you surely will realize that we have started right out at a very high point in our revelations. Before reading any further, it would be well for you to ask your Self: Why am I reading this book anyway? Beloved, you are reading these very words for the fulfillment of a definite purpose. Yes, it is for the fulfillment of the most important purpose of your Life and experience that you are right now engaged in the exploration and investigation of these Truths. It definitely is for a fulfillment of purpose that these words are being written. It is no mere happenstance that this book has come to your attention and that you are reading it this very moment. And I *know* that the purpose of this book is to be fulfilled in and as your Life, your activity, and your entire experience. In short, my purpose in writing this book and your purpose in reading it are one and the same purpose. The Consciousness that writes these Absolute Truths is the same Consciousness that reads them—and we make no compromise with duality.

From the foregoing statements, you can perceive that this is not just another book on Truth that is to be read. Neither is this just another book that is being written. Rather, it is that every Truth revealed as this book is to be — and is being — experienced. And we are both the experience and the One who experiences. Truly, we are one inseparable Consciousness because there is no such thing as separate consciousnesses.

The title of this book is *The Ultimate Awareness, an Eternal Constant.* The purpose of this book is that the complete consciousness, or awareness, of all that we *are* may be revealed, perceived, and experienced.

You will note the word *Constant* in the title of this book. This word *Constant* is of supreme importance for all of us. All too often, it *seems* that we ascend to the most glorious heights of enlightened awareness, only to seem to descend to that which appears to be the deepest darkness and gloom. As we continue, we will realize more the importance of the words *Constant, constantly,* and *Constancy.*

Now, there is one more important fact to perceive, and then we shall go into the primary Truths revealed within these pages.

You are not reading these words in order to learn anything from another or to be taught anything *by* another. There is just one complete awareness of being, and this Consciousness is equal everywhere and as every one of us. That which can be learned can also be forgotten; that which can be taught can be forgotten, but that which is experienced can *never* be forgotten. Why is this true? It is true because that which we experienced is our own Consciousness, and never can we forget, or be separated from, our own

Consciousness. There is nothing isolated in or as our Consciousness. So there can never be a genuine experience that is a separate, isolated experience. Once we consciously experience *being* what we genuinely are, we can never forget what we are. Neither can we ever be separated from the Consciousness that we are. This Consciousness that we are is an eternal, *constant* Consciousness.

We have heard about having a God-experience. What is this God-experience? Who is the "experiencer"? Can any supposedly separate one have a God-experience? Would it not have to be God, the experience, being the One who experienced? Wouldn't it have to be God being both the experience and the experiencer? There is but one Consciousness, and this one is God being conscious. Now, you are conscious, and there is nothing that can be conscious but Consciousness. When you are fully aware of being conscious *only* as the God-Consciousness being conscious, *every* experience is a God-experience. It is God experiencing being God, as all there is of the Identity that you are.

Sometimes we hold classes in the Ultimate. Those who attend these classes realize that they are *not* being taught. Every Truth that is revealed during our class sessions is revealed as the Consciousness of those who attend the class. In other words, it is all Self-revelation. Thus, these classes are being *experienced* rather than being taught. This is why the

Truths revealed during these sessions are never forgotten.

You see, Self-revelation is an experience. It is Consciousness *experiencing* being what It—Consciousness—*is*. No one can ever be separated from the Consciousness that he is. Hence, no one can lose or forget the revelations that are Self-revealed. This fact is why the class continues on and on as the experience of those who attend. Conscious Self-revelation is a continuous experience. This, Beloved, is a God-experience. It is Consciousness—God—being the experience, and it is Consciousness being the Identity who is the experiencer.

It is in this same way that this book is to be read and contemplated. To read, to contemplate, and to consciously perceive the Truths revealed herein is to truly experience these Truths. Moreover, it means that you are to experience *being* every Truth that you read. This is truly a God-experience, and there is neither beginning nor ending to this glorious Self-revelatory experience. It is all the Consciousness which is God, experiencing *being* just what God is, and nothing else.

Most of us have considered ourselves "seekers" after the Truth. We have searched and searched for God, or so we have believed. Some of us still seem to be. Now let us perceive that we are at the end of the seeming, endless search. Let us *consciously be* the Truth that we seemed to have been seeking. Our search has never been what it appeared to be. All we have ever even seemed to seek is to be fully aware of being our own God-Self. The paradox is that we only had to return—turn again—to the God-conscious Self that we have forever been, in order to perceive and experience *being* that which we imagined we were seeking.

It is true that for most of us it has seemed necessary to seek and seek and seek. For some of us, the search has appeared to be very long and even arduous. But it is encouraging to note that recently, the God I AM Self is being perceived and experienced more and more quickly. Once we have discovered and experienced *being* the Self that we are—and have always been—we clearly realize that, actually, that which we have misinterpreted as seeking was merely the God-Identity that we are, asserting Its— or His—I AM Identity to be our *only* Identity.

But there is another aspect of this subject that should be understood. No longer do we turn to teachers, leaders, masters, gurus, etc., for instruction. We now know that the very fallacy of imagining that we could be taught that which we already knew, and knew our Self to be, has seemed to delay our own Self-revelation. There is a point beyond all so-called teaching, following masters, leaders, and the like. This point is realized and manifested when we begin to experience Self-revelation. Of course, we may continue to attend classes, lectures, but our attendance is not for the purpose of being instructed. Rather, it is for the sheer joy of experiencing the indivisible Oneness that is evidenced so gloriously during the class.

Wonderful things take place during classes when the Consciousness of those who attend is far beyond any teacher or pupil misconception. Once we have reached the glorious experience of Self-revelation, we know, and we *know* that we know. Beyond any doubt, we know that always we have been, and forever we shall be, all that we have seemed to be seeking. But we also know that no one can teach our Self *to* us. No one can lead us to discover our Self. The seeming search is over. We have merely rediscovered that which we knew, and knew our Self to be, before the illusion called birth seemed to overtake us.

Does this mean the end of revelation? No! Quite the contrary is true. The revelations are ever greater and more glorious, but it is all Self-revealed. Yes, it is the Self-revealing Itself to the Self, *as* the I AM Self that we have eternally been, are now, and will eternally be.

It has been said that from beginning to end the Bible is a history of man. From an orthodox standpoint, this appears to be true. But actually, it is very far from being the truth. From Genesis through the Book of Revelation, the Bible depicts assumptive man's search for his complete, Self-conscious Being. It is *not* a matter of seeking a God outside of, or other than, our own God-conscious Self. Let us realize right here that God, being conscious, is our *only* Consciousness that we exist. Nonetheless, the Bible, from beginning to end, is a portrayal of you, of me, of everyone who exists. But particularly it depicts those of us who have—at first dimly—perceived the Absolute Truth that we are, although we have seemingly sought along many paths until we have found the way. Once we have found the way, we perceive that *we are the way*. It is no wonder that Jesus could so confidently say, "I am the way." We, too, can now say, "I am the way." Having discovered the Self, through Self-revelation, we know that the only way to know the God I Am Self is through Self-revelation. There is no other way.

Now, here we are at the end of the seeming search—the Book of Revelation, the Ultimate, or your Self-revealed. As stated in the beginning of this book, we call our way *The Ultimate, Your Self Revealed*. And, Beloved, here we are. We are arriving, or we *have* arrived, at the Ultimate, as revealed in the last book of our Bible.

There is yet another fact that should now be considered concerning your seeming search for the God I Am Self that you are. If you had not already been this God-Self before the search began, you would never have looked at the Bible. Never would you have gone inside a church. You would not have studied metaphysics, and never would you have gone on to the study of the Absolute. Certain it is that you would not be reading this book right now. It is only because you inherently knew what you were—

and are—all the while, that you even considered a search to rediscover that which you somehow knew your Self to be.

Now it is clear that your purpose in reading this book is the complete Self-revelation of what we are and *why* we are that which we are. We are to know, and to be *consciously* complete as *all* that we are. Beloved, we are so much more, so much greater than we have seemed to realize ourselves to be.

Let us sometimes, just for the sheer, infinite joy of it, go outside and gaze into the heavens—the Universe. We cannot imagine a barrier where our Consciousness comes to an end and the heavens begin. Let us question, "Where do I leave off, and where do the heavens begin?" Let us ask, "Where do the heavens end, and where does the planet Earth begin?" Let us just consider the fact that if we were on the planet Venus, to us this planet Earth would be the heavens—the sky. It is in this way that we actually begin to "feel," to sense and to be aware of, our infinite, boundless Nature. This is Self-revelation. This is the Self-revealed *to* the Self *as* the Self. This is the Ultimate Awareness that we genuinely *are*.

In Webster's unabridged dictionary, we find the following definition of *Ultimate*: "... incapable of further analysis, division, or separation." When we are fully aware of the fact that the boundless Universe—God—really is our entirety, and thus we *are* the boundless Infinity, we are beyond all so-called human analysis. We are beyond reasoning, thinking, cause and effect, birth, change, age, death. We are beyond *any* illusion of separateness or division. We are beyond any deception of "otherness." We know that there is One alone and that we are that One because there is nothing else, or other, for us to be.

Once we are fully aware of being the universal, indivisible Allness that we are, it is impossible for us to even consider ourselves to be separate persons. We could not possibly believe that we were followers or leaders, students or teachers, etc. We know that it is impossible that God, the Infinite All, could be any less complete, less total, less entire, as any one of us than as all of us. As we gaze into the heavens, we could not be aware of persons. The so-called little "I" person simply disappears in the glorious perception of our Oneness, our Allness, our indivisibility, our Totality. Now it is clear why there could be no teacher, no student, no leader, and no followers of the Ultimate.

The message is completely impersonal, and the messenger is also impersonal. The message and the messenger are one and the same. You are just as much the message as am I. You are just as much the messenger as am I. *The Ultimate Awareness is equally present as the Entirety that is each and every one of us.* What is the message that is the messenger? *You* are the Ultimate. *You* are beyond all duality. *You* are the universal All, being All. *You* are Infinity being infinite. *You* are Equality being equal. *You* are infinite

Consciousness being infinitely conscious. *You* are infinite, eternal Mind being intelligent. Above all, *you* are eternal, perfect, constant Love being eternally, constantly loving. Never again will you even *seem* to limit your wonderful, boundless Self.

Throughout the ages, so-called man has been fascinated by the heavens. This is why astrology is supposed to extend back so far into that which is called the history of man. (Oh, of course, there is no time, but that is the way it appears to be.) Primitive man considered the sun, the moon, the stars, the waves, and even the winds to be gods. And many of the ancient myths refer to the gods of the sun, the moon, the stars, the winds, etc. It is also interesting to note so-called man's intense desire to rise above the Earth and into the heavens.

Why should there be this great interest in so-called space? The answer is very simple. Inherently, man has known that he was not confined to Earth, nor was he circumscribed by so-called boundaries of the Earth planet. Inherently he has known that actually he was—and is—the boundless, free Universe Itself. Even in that which is called the human effort to rise ever higher into the heavens, there is this inherent urge to rediscover his completely free, boundless Self.

It is interesting to see that even assumptive man senses the fact that he is boundless and unconfined. But of course, *our* seeming search is not at all based upon the false premise of "man with breath in his nostrils." We, for the most part, have not sought to rediscover our God-Self from the so-called human or scientific standpoint. Rather, we have based all of our seeking upon the spiritual basis. Nonetheless, our desire to truly know our limitless, infinite Self is the *absolute Fact* behind and beyond the seeming search of assumptive man. All of us seem to have been seeking to discover, to perceive, and finally to *be* the boundless Infinitude which is God being All, All being God. Let us then consider the heavens, and as we gaze into the boundless Infinity which is God, we can realize that *we* are just what this limitless Universe *is*, and nothing else or other.

Now, the question may arise, "But is this practical? Does it work in and as our daily experience and our bodies?" Indeed, the Ultimate Absolute way is practical. We do experience the manifestation of Its omnipotent activity in and as our daily experience and as the entirety of the body. Do we give the body a treatment? Do we concentrate our attention upon the body or its activity? Indeed, we do no such thing. Rather, we instantly "consider the heavens."

We perceive the fact that the *only* Substance that exists, to be in Form, is the one Indivisible Substance, which is this boundless Universe. We also realize that the *only* Activity there is, or can be, is the infinite, perfect, inseparable, omnipresent Activity, which is God in action. (Oh, there is infinite Power in this contemplation. The universal Presence is the universal Power.) Thus, we realize that the only

Substance, the only Activity, we can have or be is the eternal, immutable Substance in constant action, which is Infinitude, God, in action. And of course, this means that the *only* Body we have, or are, *has* to be this eternal, ever-enduring Omniaction, being active *as* the *one universal, indivisible, ever-perfect Substance, which is the Body, right here and now.*

Therefore, your Body is perfect, eternal, imperishable, indestructible. Consider the indestructibility that is this Universe and perceive how perfect It has to be — and to remain — in order to endure eternally. Just consider that It is the *only* Substance and that It is beginningless, changeless, and endless. Realizing that the universal, omniactive Substance is eternal, beginningless, changeless, and endless — *and that this is the only Substance in existence* — you will readily perceive that your omniactive Substance has to be omniactive, beginningless, changeless, and endless. In this way, you will be aware of the fact that your Substance is birthless, ageless, changeless, deathless. Actually, you do not have to focus your attention on the Body at all. You see, the Body *is* the very Consciousness that you are, aware of being just what you are conscious of being.

Now that you know what Body is, you perceive that whatever you are aware of being, the Body is aware of being. Is this practical? Indeed so. And every day brings reports that verify the practicality of this Ultimate perception. There is indeed constant proof of the manifestation of the Truth we are perceiving.

Also, now let us say that the very same Truth that manifests Itself as perfect, omniactive Body also manifests Itself as perfect, omniactive business and as all the experience of our daily affairs.

We have spoken of the fact that the Bible depicts man's seeming search for his own completeness, his own Self. And we have mentioned the fact that this Completeness may be easily realized when we "consider the heavens." (Incidentally, this means to keep the Mind stayed on God.) There are many citations in the Bible that point up this fact. Just now, we will mention only a few of these citations. But consider the Psalmist, David, under the stars, contemplating the boundless Heavens. Is it surprising that he sang:

> Whither shall I go from thy spirit? or whither shall I flee from thy presence? If I ascend up into heaven, thou art there: if I make my bed in hell, behold, thou art there. If I take the wings of the morning, and dwell in the uttermost parts of the sea; even there shall thy hand lead me, and thy right hand shall hold me (Ps. 139:7-10).

Then there is the portrayal of the wise men who followed the star of Bethlehem:

> When they had heard the king, they departed, and lo, the star, which they saw in the east, went before them, till it came and stood over where the young child was. When they saw the star, they rejoiced with exceeding great joy (Matt. 2:9-10).

This reported episode, of course, is symbolic, simply portraying the fact that it is the contemplation of boundless Infinitude, the Universe Itself, that reveals the Christ—or Truth—which is the Consciousness that comprises all there is of us.

There really is great significance for us in this revelation. As you know, the number *three* is used in our Bible again and again as a symbol for Completeness. (Whenever the number *three* is mentioned in the Bible, it would be well to investigate the Completeness which it portrays.)

It is noteworthy that the wise men saw the star —Light—and began their search for the complete revelation of Man—the Christ, the Light. For that matter, symbolically is this not the case with all of us? Didn't we first glimpse the Light? Didn't we begin our seeming search for the complete revelation of our Christ-Being? Didn't we also continue our journey until we discovered the Christ, the Light, Man, the Self? Is this not the way it has *appeared* to be with every one of us? And when we really have arrived at the Ultimate Absolute discovery, which is Completeness, we do perceive that the Christ-Light is what we are, what we always have been, and what we everlastingly will be.

Every one of us who perceives the star, the Light, and pursues it is destined to discover the Christ, heavenly Light, which is our Entirety. Of course, the significance of all of this is the fact that once we discover that the Infinite is all there is of us, we also perceive that the Infinite is the eternal Christ that is Man. Man, the boundless Infinite All, is the Christ. The Christ is God, Infinitude, being Man.

Now, it is clear that the Light which is the Christ-Man is unconfined and uncontained. It is as universal as is God, for it *is* God. This, Beloved, is that which is seen when, in illumination, we see the Universe as Light. The Christ—all there is of you or of anyone—is infinite, boundless Light. The Christ, Man, is God; God is the Christ-Man. It is God, of whom the Bible speaks as being Light, and "in him there is no darkness at all."

Never hesitate to admit this fact *to* your Self, *as* your Self. Is it any wonder that Jesus said, "Ye are the light of the world"? Yes, you are the Christ-Light because the Light is *you*. Now you can joyously say:

> I am the Christ; I am the Light; I am the Mind
> that was—and is—in Christ Jesus. I am the Light,
> for the Light is all there is of the *I* that I am.

Now you perceive that the eternal Christ that is this Christ-Light comprises all there is of you. This signifies that the boundless Light that you are is the birthless, changeless, deathless Christ, which is God, being Man. Jesus was, and *is*, the infinite Christ-Light. Nonetheless, Jesus was, and *is*, an eternal Identity. In this same way, you are the boundless, eternal Christ-Light, but you are also an eternal Identity. Jesus' Eternality is his Infinity; his Infinity is his Eternality. Your Eternality is your Infinity, and your Infinity is your Eternality. There is neither time nor space. There is only Eternity; there is only Infinity. Eternity and Infinity are one and the same.

You will recall that Jesus said, "Follow thou me." Well, he certainly did not mean that we were to follow a personal Jesus. He did mean that until we are fully aware that we are the complete, universal Christ-Light, we are to continue to pursue the Light, the star, the Christ. In *The Gospel According to Thomas*, Jesus' meaning is clarified when he says, "Let him who seeks not cease seeking until he has found." This is what Jesus meant when he said, "Follow thou me."

Now, of course, we are never going to discover what we are until we are through thinking, reasoning, or concentrating in meditation. We will never discover our infinite Allness by making any effort with the so-called born human mind. The *only* way in which the full Light dawns is in being full open Consciousness.

Right here, the word *consider* is important. When we are considering something that already *is*, we are not trying—or making an effort—to make it *become* that which it is. It requires no effort to consider the heavens. This effortless consideration is being full open Consciousness, and in reading the Truths herein presented, you will truly perceive the infinite, eternal Entirety that you are, through *being* full open Consciousness.

There is one point that is of tremendous importance to your being "full open." Do not try to *interpret* the words you read here. These words cannot be interpreted. Any attempt to do so would be an effort of the so-called born mind and could only lead to confusion and frustration.

You have heard the expression "Keep an open mind about this." Well, the significance behind and beyond this statement is that it is well to simply read and let the words flow as they will. If the words make no sense to you, pay no attention. Suddenly, if the Consciousness is full open, you will clearly understand some point that hitherto seemed obscure or senseless. Then the Light will dawn more brightly and faster as you go along. Before you have completed reading the book, you are very apt to experience what we call a "breakthrough." This word *breakthrough* means that you suddenly see your Self, everyone, and everything the way it *is* rather than the way it *seems* to be. (We will have more to say about this word *breakthrough* later in this book.)

Chapter II

Consciousness

Let us now consider the important word *Consciousness*. We know that Consciousness is *awareness*. We are conscious; thus, we are aware of being, or existing. Thus, our Consciousness is our awareness of being. But let us ask, "What is Consciousness aware of being?" Well, Consciousness is aware of being just what It *is* and nothing else. Consciousness does not exist as dense, solid, separate pieces, or particles, of matter. It is impossible for Consciousness to be aware of matter because Consciousness is *not* matter. And remember, Consciousness is only aware of that which It *is*. There is no temporary Consciousness; thus, Consciousness cannot be a temporary Substance. Yes, Consciousness is Substance, but Consciousness, being eternal, constant, changeless, is not, and cannot be, an awareness of being a temporary substance that is constantly being interrupted by birth and death.

It does not matter in what form Consciousness may exist—Consciousness is aware of *being* that Substance, that Form, and that Activity. For instance, the *only* Substance existing in that form called tree is Consciousness aware of being what It *is* as *that* tree. Consciousness, being complete as whatever It *is*, is aware of being the complete tree. Consciousness is aware of being the seed, the roots, the trunk, every branch, leaf, fruit, or flower that comprises that tree. And, Beloved, *this is the Consciousness that is the Substance, Form, and Activity that is the tree, aware of being the tree*. So you can perceive that the tree is aware of being just what it is.

Nonetheless, Consciousness, aware of being eternal, is aware of being the eternal Substance, Form, and Activity that is the tree. And because Consciousness cannot be aware of any interruption in Its being, Its awareness of existing as that tree cannot be interrupted by beginning or ending of Itself *as* that tree. Thus, the tree cannot be aware of beginning or ending. Of course, it *appears* to us that the seed is first; then the tree grows from the seed; then come the branches, the blossoms, the fruit, or whatever comprises the tree.

Beloved, it only *appears* to be this way because we apparently do not see things as they genuinely are. It is only when we are illumined to the point of the "breakthrough" that we see the eternal, ever-present, complete tree, forever existing as the glorious, beginningless, immutable, endless Completeness that it is.

In the Bible we read, "Every hair of your head is numbered." There is tremendous significance in this statement. Every branch, every leaf of every tree exists, and is, as eternal as is the tree itself. There is never one more or one less leaf existing as that tree.

There is never one more or one less branch, blossom, nut, orange, etc. The tree is constantly and eternally complete as just what it is and *only* what it is. Certainly it seems to most of us that the leaves come and go. They appear as new, fresh leaves, and then they seem to dry, fall, and disappear. But really the leaves of the tree are as eternal and constant as is the tree itself. Why is this true? It is true because each leaf of the tree *is* the tree. Each leaf of the tree is the body of the tree, even as the body of the tree is each leaf of the tree. Consciousness is aware of being the tree, the body of the tree, the seed, the trunk, the branches, the leaves, and all that exists as the eternal, immutable, imperishable tree.

Again, Consciousness is aware of being the eternal, changeless, constant Substance that It *is*, as every iota, every aspect, of that tree. Furthermore, It never began to be aware of being the tree, nor does It ever end being aware of the fact that It is the tree.

Now, how temporary is the tree? How temporary is every branch, leaf, etc., that comprise the tree? The tree knows nothing of leaves that come and go, of branches that break and fall, etc. The tree is simply aware of being Itself as *All* that it is and as the eternal Completeness that it is.

Who or what does appear to be aware of leaves, branches, etc., that come and go? Since the appearance of change, deterioration, and death is *not* the Consciousness that is the tree, it has to be our false concept of the tree. The tree remains exactly what it is, and *All* that it is, no matter how imperfectly we seem to see it. So the seeming deterioration, death, etc., is not the Consciousness—Substance—that is the tree. If there were such a thing as deterioration, death, and the like, it would have to be our own awareness of the tree. So the apparent constant coming and going of the leaves, branches, etc., is merely our seemingly imperfect way of seeing, or perceiving, the tree.

Let us have a simile that may help to clarify this important point. For instance, we may watch a loved one or a friend board a huge plane. We see the plane taxi along and finally take off. Now, very quickly it begins to appear to diminish in size as far as our vision is concerned. Finally, it seems to be a small dot in the sky. And at last, it seems to have completely disappeared. Now, has the plane or anyone on that plane diminished or shrunk? Have they disappeared because we no longer see them? Isn't the plane, complete with crew and passengers, just the same as it was when it left the ground? Indeed so. If the body of the plane had diminished and disappeared, wouldn't the body of everyone on that plane have had to diminish and disappear?

Of course, we know that the plane and all who boarded remain the same. So we are not deceived by the appearance of a diminishing or disappearing plane. But we do seem to be deceived by the appearance of changing, deteriorating, disappearing leaves, branches, etc., of the tree. Why should this be? It is because we do not seem to know that the tree is an ever-complete Existent and that It does not begin, change, or end. We seem to falsely believe that everything and everyone has to begin, to change, to become imperfect, to deteriorate, and to end, or die.

In a recent issue of *Scientific American*, there is an article by Richard L. Gregory. Mr. Gregory is chairman of the Department of Machine Intelligence and Perception at the University of Edinburgh. In reading this article, it becomes apparent that we seem to see just what we *expect* to see. It is an exceedingly interesting article and one that is well worth reading. In any event, the important fact is significant pertaining to the Truth we have just been reading.

When we really *see* the tree, when we really *see* the eternal Heaven that *is here, now, and evermore*, we perceive that nothing ever begins (is born) or ends (dies) here. In this perception, we see the tree as it eternally, constantly is. Thus *we know, and we know that we know, the genuine nature of all Existence.*

Now, one might ask whether or not there is any biblical authority for the Truths we have just been discussing. Indeed, there is biblical authority. In fact, every Truth we can ever write, speak, or read is presented within the pages of our beloved Bible. We only have to recognize these Truths when we discover and read them. This recognition, of course, requires knowledge of the Absolute Ultimate. Once we are aware of being the Mind that *is* all

Intelligence, thus all knowledge, we instantly recognize any absolute statement of Truth wherever we find It.

Let us now speak of the Absolute Truth that the tree—everything and everyone—is. Let us realize that everything and everyone remains eternally complete as just what it *is*. Nothing is ever added to this Completeness, nor can anything ever disappear from the Completeness that exists as everything and everyone. In Matthew 10:30, we read, "But the very hairs of your head are all numbered." We also find this absolute statement of Truth—eternal Completeness—in Luke 12:7. Luke makes a very terse and definite statement of eternal Completeness when he states, "But even the very hairs of your head are all numbered."

This, Beloved, leaves no doubt at all of the fact that Jesus was, and is, fully aware of the eternal existence of everything that is the tree, the blade of grass, or of anything that exists, including the Body. Actually, if Consciousness in and as Form does exist as something called cells, atoms, etc., of the Body, there could never be one more or one less cell, atom, etc. There is a divine, orderly economy, as stated in the 1966 class, and this divine economy precludes the possibility that *any* aspect of the Body can either multiply or diminish.

We have stated that the complete Essence of all Substance (Consciousness) existing as Form is, and remains, forever changeless. Among the statements in our Bible that verify this Truth, we find, "Neither shalt thou swear by thy head, because thou canst not make one hair white or black" (Matt. 5:36). Obviously Jesus was, and *is*, fully aware of the Completeness that is eternal and of the complete immutability that is eternal.

So when we actually see things as they are, we also see everything as eternal, perfect, complete, and changeless. And pertaining to this Body right here, we must really *know* just what this Body genuinely is. Otherwise, we are going to continue to *appear* to have bodies that are born, that change, mature, deteriorate, age, and end, or die.

The Body does not begin. It is not born. The Body does not change, become imperfect, deteriorate, age, die, or end. The Body consists of Consciousness aware of being what It is, and *All that It is*, as this Body. Nothing is ever added to, or subtracted from, this Body. Even the form of this Body remains the same without one iota of change. Not one hair of the head comes or goes.

Now, where and what is this appearance of body that seems to us to be born, to change, to decay, to age, and to die? It is only in our fallacious way of "seeing" and believing this Body to be other than It is. As stated before, we see—yes, we appear to experience—just what we expect to see and to experience. Oh, yes, we do appear to expect the Body to grow, to mature, to age, to become imperfect, to deteriorate, and to die. And of course, all of this misconception stems from the delusion that the Body is born, that it begins.

Nonetheless, this eternal Body knows *only* what it is. It consists of the Consciousness that *you* are, aware of being what you are, and *only* what you are. The genuine and *only* Body is impervious to and completely unaffected by—and above all, immune to—our seeming misconceptions about It.

It knows nothing at all of our imperfect way of seeing It. Actually, this Body is simply the awareness of the genuine and *only* Consciousness that you are, aware of what the Body is, and of *being* this Body that *is*. Body is eternal, constant, immutable Consciousness in Form. But Consciousness is also Life, Mind, Intelligence, Love. So Body consists of conscious, eternal, immutable Intelligence, Love. It consists of living Mind, or Intelligence.

The importance of knowing just what the Body is cannot be over-emphasized. This is true because the Consciousness that you *are*, knowing what the Body *is*, actually is the Substance, the Activity, the Form, the *manifestation* of the Body, right here and now.

Always bear in Mind, though, that Consciousness is eternal, infinite, boundless, inseparable, universal, omnipotent Omnipresence. Indeed, this Body is *ever-present* living, loving, conscious Mind, Intelligence, in Form. Let us go all the way and perceive that the Body is boundless, infinite, universal, omnipotent, omnipresent, eternal God in and *as* Form and Activity.

The Body is—and has to be—as eternal and as perfect as is God because *God is the Body; thus, the Body is God.* This, Beloved, is why the Body cannot begin, change, or end. You will find that throughout these pages we will again and again return to this aspect of our eternal Being—Identity—called Body.

Chapter III

Consciousness Focalized

Let us again consider the word *Consciousness*. We have said that Consciousness is aware of being what It is, and all that It is. We know that the omnipresent Substance which is Consciousness is everywhere; we know that this omnipresent Consciousness is a *constant*, omniactive Substance and that It is without a vacuum and without an interruption.

Consciousness is constantly, eternally aware of being what It is at any specific focal point. But Consciousness is also aware of being *where* It is. This is like the eddies in and as the boundless Ocean of living Light, as it was revealed in the first of our 1966 classes. The eddy is merely a focal point, or focalization, of the infinite, surging, ever-flowing Light that *is* this Universe, Infinity. It is in this same way that the infinite, omniactive Consciousness that *you are* is focalized right here and right now.

But this is not all; the boundless, living Consciousness that you are is aware that there is a specific, as well as universal, purpose in being focalized here. Furthermore, the infinite, intelligent Consciousness that you are — focalized right here and now — is aware of just what the purpose is in being focalized here, now. But most important of all is the fact that this Consciousness is aware of fulfilling—or of being the fulfillment of—Its purpose in being focalized right here, right now.

Of course, you realize that we are not speaking of so-called time or space. Again, there is neither time nor space. Actually, the words *here* and *now* merely denote the focalization of your Consciousness being the *here* and the *now* of your specific fulfillment of purpose. Wherever and whenever your attention is focalized is "here and now" as far as you are concerned. And this absolute, infinite, yet focalized, Truth is the *power of all your seeing, and being that which you see.* The focalization is never something or some activity that is separate from, or other than, the boundless Infinity that is being focalized.

It is of the utmost importance that you *always realize* that it is the infinite, universal Consciousness that you are that is focalized wherever your attention is focused. You see, this realization of being the boundless *All* is the power of the entire perception.

Chapter IV

Purpose Fulfilled as Body

There is a purpose that is fulfilled by the Consciousness that you are, aware of *being* the Body. And because the universal Consciousness that you are is focalized *as* this Body, the Body Itself is aware of Its purpose in being. It—the Body—is also aware of being the fulfillment of Its purpose in being.

We know that there is no little isolated identity separate from, or other than, the boundless, universal I AM that is God. We also know that there is no little isolated body that is separate from, or other than, the universal Substance, Body, that is God. In this same way, there is no little isolated purpose to be fulfilled that is separate from, or other than, God in action, which, of course, is the Infinite All fulfillment of purpose. Therefore, there is no little isolated fulfillment of purpose that is separate from, or other than, the universal fulfillment of purpose.

Often it seems that our very existence is purposeless. Again, it may appear that we are not successfully or completely fulfilling some specific purpose. The very moment we realize that it is all God, the universal Consciousness, *aware of being the complete fulfillment of Its purpose,* we know just what our purpose in being focalized is. We also know that we are successfully and completely being the fulfillment of our purpose in being, just by consciously existing.

All activity, whether it be bodily activity, business activity, professional activity, or whatever, is inseparable from the Omniaction which is God — the boundless Universe — actively, intelligently, completely, successfully fulfilling Its purpose. We cannot consider conscious, living Intelligence being active as business, profession, or whatever as though It were separate from, or other than, this living, conscious Intelligence being active as our bodily activity. Just as surely as we are not clear on this point, we will surely consider this Body to be something separate from, or other than, the universal Body. Thus, we will be deluded into believing that we have a separate activity of our own. Right here is where, and why, we seem to get into trouble.

All of these supposedly physical functions are really spiritual activities — or infinite Intelligence — being active. These spiritual functions are really Consciousness fulfilling Its purpose, infinitely as well as specifically. When we perceive that a body of matter simply does not exist, then we also see that there is no born or material body that can be active. And, beloved One, instantly we *know* that we do not have, and are not, a born body. We are completely free from every so-called law that is supposed to govern the supposedly born body. This means that we are completely free from all the fallacious laws of change, illness, imperfection, infection, age, deterioration, and death. Oh, how wonderful it is to realize that because our kingdom is not of this world, we are not subject to one single cruel, fallacious law of the seeming world of birth, of imperfection, age, and death.

It is this seemingly troublesome *appearance* of a born body that appears to be a separate substance in form, with a separate activity of its own. It is this same false appearance of body that seems to be independent from, and other than, the infinite, boundless, indivisible All-Substance in ceaseless action. There can no more be separate activity than there can be a separate substance. The activity is the Substance, the activity is the Form; even as the Substance, the Form, is the Activity.

Often we have discussed the fact that there is one breath and one who breathes. This boundless Universe is a living, breathing, active Substance. And breath, or the activity of breathing, is a necessary fulfillment of purpose of Life Itself. Thus, this Universe does breathe. Breathing is an essential fulfillment of the universal purpose of eternal, omnipresent Life Itself. Universal Life is alive. And breathing is necessary in order that conscious, intelligent, loving Life be—and remain—eternally alive. You can no more separate the focalized fulfillment of your Life than you can separate the eddy from the water that forms it.

Now, if you are tempted to believe that you are not fulfilling any purpose in being, you can realize that every breath you take is an important and essential fulfillment of the universal purpose. True it is that the breathing that goes on as this bodily activity *is* the universal purpose fulfilling Itself, but it is the universal breath fulfilling its purpose, focalized right here and now, as your breathing. Nonetheless, it is still the infinite, indivisible All— God—who breathes as *your* very breathing. It is small wonder that the poet said that God was "closer than breathing." In any event, you can see that you could not exist, you could not be conscious or alive, if you were not the universal All, fulfilling Its purpose in being *you*.

We are not going to talk about a kind of body that does not exist. But we now have to use some very misleading words. These words are necessary in order to further perceive just how it is, and why it is, that this Body is a fulfillment of a universal purpose. We are speaking now of this focalization of the universal All that you call your Body, right here and now. As you know, we are supposed to have organs, cells, etc., in order to be alive. Behind and beyond *every* so-called organ, cell, etc., there really is Substance in and as Form. And this Substance in Form is necessary to the Completeness that is this Body. This is why it is said that nothing is ever added to or subtracted from this Body.

It seems that teeth present quite a problem for many of us. In the first place, the body is supposed to be toothless, incomplete, at birth. And if one lives to old age, the body is supposed to be incomplete—toothless—when we die. Indeed, this is a terrible way to talk or to write. Nevertheless, this is the fallacious law that so-called born man appears to be under. The false picture is indeed an atrocious lie. But suppose that it does seem that the teeth are deteriorating and disappearing. Suppose that some or all of the teeth *seem* to be missing. What are we to perceive in such a dire appearance of incompleteness? (Incidentally, I have just read a testimonial or report in which it was stated that many teeth that were apparently decayed or missing were replaced naturally, and the writer reported that he now has a full and complete complement of teeth. Isn't this wonderful!)

Well, this Body is ever-present Consciousness, aware of being what It is and all that It is. Furthermore, this Body is aware of being where It belongs, and where It is, as the perfect, eternal *complete* Substance in Form which is every tooth, every so-called organ, every hair of the head. *There is no temporary Substance, and there is no temporal Substance in Form*, whether it be called teeth, hair, cells, atoms, or by any other name.

Consciousness is aware of being what It is at every focal point of Itself. Consciousness is aware of being what It is at the focal point called every tooth, every hair of the head, every cell, organ, or whatever Consciousness in Form may be called. Consciousness is aware of being the fulfillment of Its purpose right where It is, and as just what It is. Consciousness is aware of being eternal, immutable, indestructible, imperishable, complete, whole, constant *as* every tooth, every so-called aspect that is this eternal, perfect Body.

It is not at all important what *any* Substance in Form may be named by assumptive man or how it may appear to the false sense of vision of "man with breath in his nostrils." The incontrovertible fact remains:

All Substance is beginningless, changeless, endless, imperishable, indestructible, Absolute Perfection in and as Form and Activity.

Chapter V

Vision

Often we have discussed Vision, and often we have written pertaining to the fulfillment of purpose called Vision. However, as fresh and new revelations occur, we must present them as they are revealed. The revelations themselves are a definite fulfillment of purpose.

We have said that Vision is Consciousness and that conscious perception, or Consciousness perceiving, is Vision, and this is indeed true. But Consciousness is Substance. This being true, *Vision is Substance: it is the very Substance that comprises the eye itself.* But the Substance that is Vision is not confined to the eye or eyes. *Seeing* is Consciousness actively perceiving, and Consciousness seeing is Consciousness actively fulfilling Its purpose as seeing.

No, the Substance which is Vision is *not* confined to the eyes. Actually, It is entirely unconfined. We see with and *as* the Substance that is the Body. Furthermore, we see with and *as* all the *infinite, boundless Substance — Consciousness — that we are.*

Vision is everywhere, everywhere equally the same. It is conscious Mind (Intelligence) *actively* perceiving and discriminating. It is conscious Mind in the act of knowing the Substance and Activity of that which It is seeing. This is discrimination.

Vision is infinite, intelligent, conscious perception, fulfilling Its infinite purpose by perceiving. But it is this same boundless, omnipresent, conscious perception that is focalized right here and now as the Body, the Vision that you are, and that is the very Substance in Form that you may call your eyes.

The purpose of Vision is to see. Vision is always constantly, consciously fulfilling Its purpose by seeing. There can be no imperfect Vision, for there is no imperfect, or incomplete, Consciousness—God. There is no imperfect Consciousness being Vision, so there is no imperfect awareness of seeing. No one *has* Vision. Rather, Vision is something that we *are*. Beloved, all there is of that which you call Vision is your active awareness of seeing and of intelligently discriminating. For instance, when we are seeing a tree, we know that what we see is the tree and not a house, a bird, etc. This is discrimination, or Intelligence discriminating as to form, color, etc.

Do you ask why it is that it seems that you see only with, or through, the eyes? It is only because your awareness of seeing seems to be focalized as the eyes. This is the limitation of so-called born man and his limited misconception of Vision. But the Vision that you *are* is absolutely boundless and unlimited. Full illumination *always* reveals infinite, unconfined awareness of being to be the Consciousness that you are, seeing infinitely, perfectly, constantly, eternally. It is the universal, omnipotent, omnipresent, complete Vision that sees, and this infinite Vision sees equally everywhere.

Vision is *always* complete. Why is this true? It is true because Consciousness is always complete as what It is, and as all that It is. Yes, Consciousness is everywhere equal. And wherever there is Consciousness—and that is everywhere—there is Vision. Wherever there is Consciousness, there is the boundless I AM that you are, aware of being perfect seeing.

All that is true of Vision is also true of hearing. This is true because the seeing and the hearing are the very same Consciousness, aware of being. Now you can joyously say:

> All there is of this Vision right here and now is the Consciousness that I am, aware of seeing. All there is of this hearing right here and now is the Consciousness that I am, aware of hearing. I can only see Perfection; thus, I can only see perfectly. I can only hear Perfection; thus, I can only hear perfectly.
>
> This is true because I can only see, I can only hear, as the eternal, constant, complete, perfect Consciousness that I am. All there is of this Body is my awareness of being what I am, where I am, and of being the fulfillment of purpose which is going on as this Body.
>
> *I*—the infinite, constant *I* that I am—really am fulfilling my purpose, focalized as this everperfect, omniactive Body.

Again, let us quote from Ecclesiastes: "There is one alone, and there is not another." There is one I AM being, and there is not another. There is not another being. There is one *I* that I am and no other. There are not two of the infinite *I* that I am. There is no little born "I" that can be anyone or anything at all. *Everyone is this one indivisible I that I am, even as I am the one I that is everyone.*

There is no "I" aware of trouble, fear, or a multitude of problems. There is no "I" aware of being a perishable, destructible substance or a born, temporary, imperfect substance in form.

Chapter VI

I Am Contemplation

I am the sum total, the aggregate, that is every Truth. I am the Eternality that is eternal. I am the eternal Life that is eternally alive. I am the eternal Consciousness that is eternally conscious. I am the eternal Mind that is eternally intelligent. I am the eternal Love that is eternally loving.

I am the eternal Absolute Truth that is eternally, absolutely true. I am the eternal Truth that is Constancy. I am the eternal Truth that is Entirety, Totality, Completeness, Allness, Onliness. I am the Perfection that is perfect. I am the Immutability that is immutable. I am the Wholeness that is whole, entire, complete. I am the Inseparability that is inseparable. I am the eternal, infinite Constant that is alive. I am the eternal, constant Consciousness that is conscious. I am the infinite, eternal, constant Mind that is intelligent. I am the eternal, infinite, constant Love that is loving.

I am the evidence of the infinite, eternal, constant *I* that I am. I am the manifestation of the *I* that I am, called Man. I am the evidence of things supposedly unseen. That which I am—yes, even that which is visible to the so-called eye of assumptive man—is the evidence of the unseen *I* that I am. That which is seen, and all that can be seen, is the evidence of the seemingly invisible Life, Love, Mind (Intelligence) Consciousness that I am.

That which is visible is the evidence of the Infinity that I am. That which is visible is the evidence of the Eternality that I am. That which is visible is the evidence of the omnipresent Constancy that I am. That which is visible is the evidence of the constant Immutability that I am. That which is visible is the evidence of the eternal Perfection, the birthless, ageless, deathless Beauty that I am. That which is visible, and *only* that which is visible, is the evidence of the sum total of every universal Truth that I am.

"In my flesh shall I see God." Although not one Absolute Truth appears to be visible as the *I* that I am, actually, *every* Truth that I am really is visible — is evidenced — as all there is of the *I* that I am and as all that can be seen by the so-called eyes of seemingly born man. The visible evidence of the universal *I* that I am is the fulfillment of my purpose in being the sum total of all Truth. Without the *evidence* of the sum total of all Truth that I am, there would be no purpose fulfilled in, or by, my existence or being.

I am all Absolute Truth, being the visible evidence of all that I am. I cannot be the evidence of that which I am not. I can only be the evidence of that which I infinitely, eternally, constantly, immutably am.

The boundless, infinite Substance—Consciousness—that I am, is fulfilling Its purpose by being evident—being focalized—as this visible Body right here and now. The universal, indivisible *I* that is all Being is aware of being the evidence—focalization— of Itself right here and now as *this* Body.

All that can be visibly evidenced here is the Eternality, Perfection, Immutability, Constancy, Wholeness, Beauty, Infinity that I am.

Chapter VII

The Body Is Not an Illusion

Dear reader, I am fully aware that, to those who are not seasoned students of the Ultimate, many of the statements in the foregoing paragraphs may seem confusing, contradictory, or downright idiocy. But please bear with us and continue reading. Just let the Truths that are to follow reveal themselves as your own Consciousness. Please be assured that before you have read the last line, the last paragraph in this book, all that has been said or that is to be said will be perfectly clear, and even logical.

One statement must be made right here and now. *This Body is not an illusion.* Those who have insisted upon claiming that the Body is an illusion have seemed to deteriorate, age, become ill, and die. Let us face a few facts here. There is no Love in sickness, pain, and death. In our Bible, God speaks in this manner: "I have no pleasure in the death of him who dieth." Well, of course not. Death, if there were such an atrocity, would be completely contrary to God, who is Life Eternal.

Indeed, this Body is not an illusion. It is genuine; It is Truth; It is real. It is the infinite *I* that I am, manifested. It is the infinite Body focalized right here, right now, constantly, eternally. Nothing exists as this Body that is not the infinite, eternal, constant *I* that I am, focalized. As you can see, this Body is not an illusion. This is true because the *infinite* Body is genuine and real.

There is no presence or power existing that can compel the *I* that I am to see, touch, hear, or experience an illusory misconception of or about this Body. Nothing and no one ever deceives the *I* that I am. I can only *seem* — for a short moment in the eternal Being that I am — to deceive my Self.

"Call no man father who is upon the earth, for one is your Father, which is in heaven" (Matt. 23:9). Again and again, I return to the fact that there is no birth, thus, no born body. You will recall that in Proverbs we read about the necessity for "line upon line, precept upon precept." Many of you have said that the frequent realization of the birthless Nature of man is of the utmost importance. It is true that the supposedly born body appears to be or to become troublesome and then to die. But this is not all: the supposedly born man — life, consciousness, intelligence — that is believed to begin with the misconception (thus the birth of that which is called this body) is, of necessity, temporary.

If there were no apparent misconception, called born man, there would not even seem to be trouble or problems of *any* nature. Every problem that we appear to encounter can always be traced right to this "born man" fallacy. *But there is no birth; there is no born body*. The *only* Substance that is ever alive is Life,

Consciousness, Mind (Intelligence), Love. Substance consists of omniactive, eternal, ever-perfect, immutable, living, loving, conscious Intelligence, or Mind. And this ever-active, constant Mind is never born. It is only because the infinite, indivisible Identity does identify Itself *as* every Identity that a supposedly born separate identity can appear.

It is essential that we perceive the genuine and *only* Nature of that which we call this Body. It is necessary to realize that it is eternal, constant Life that is alive here; it is this eternal, constant Life that is *conscious* here; and this living Consciousness is Intelligence here. Above all, it is this same living, conscious Intelligence that is loving here. Of the utmost importance is the realization that this ever alive, conscious, living Intelligence is *Substance.* It is the only Substance that exists as this Body right here and now. This is the Body that has sometimes been called the Body of Spirit, or the spiritual Body.

It never occurs to us that a spiritual Body could be born. Then why should we be misled into accepting the fallacy that this eternal Body of conscious, living, intelligent Love is born? (Actually there is no misconception, nor is there a misconceiver or misperceiver.) Yes, it is eternal, infinite, living, conscious, loving Intelligence that is *consciously* alive here. It is not a conglomeration of attributes or qualities that were born into a temporary body that must sicken, age, and finally die.

57

Love is always lovely; Beauty is always beautiful; Grace is always graceful; Symmetry is always
symmetrical. All of this means that there is no born
man with a born body here at all—*but there is a body
here*. Make no mistake about this fact.

It is conscious, infinite Vision that sees here, not
a finite born vision. It is infinite Hearing that hears
right here and now, not a finite hearing limited to the
supposed ears of born man. It is universal Mind that
knows right here, not a misconception of mind,
limited to a supposed born brain. It is infinite,
eternal, perfect Substance that is in Form here, not a
suppositional born body. It is eternal, infinite, constant Substance that is whole, complete, substantial,
here and now, not a temporary, mutable, solid, dense,
born body. *And it is possible to see this eternal Substance that is in Form right here.*

The infinite Vision does not limit, obstruct, or
destroy Itself or Its "seeing." The Mind I am cannot
be compelled to know anything that does not exist.
The Vision that I am cannot be compelled to see a
distorted picture of that which exists. The Hearing I
am cannot be compelled to hear *anything* that is not
true, genuine, or anything that is false. Truth alone
exists, and Truth is all that can be heard.

The eternal Life I am cannot be compelled to be
a temporary, born life. The eternal, indestructible,
imperishable, immutable *I*-Substance I am cannot be
compelled to change, to become imperfect, deteriorate, age, and die. Neither can I ever be extinguished

or destroyed. The infinite purposefulness I am cannot be compelled to become purposeless. I am the infinite Purpose, fulfilling Itself here and now. In short, a deception called birth cannot compel the *I* that I am to see, to hear, to know, or to be anything that I am not.

Jesus knew—and knows—that Man is birthless. This fact is clearly revealed in *The Gospel According to Thomas*. During our class in Vista in 1967, we dwelt with the birthless, deathless Melchizedek. And there are many instances recorded in our Bible of the birthless, deathless Nature of Man. Indeed, Jesus does know that there is no birth, and he intends that we also shall know this Truth.

Jesus knew that no born man was his father, but he also knew that no born woman was his mother. To many students, this may seem to be a shocking statement. However, it is absolutely true. Jesus even knew that he did not have born brothers. You will find proof of these statements in our Bible:

> While he yet talked to the people, behold, his mother and his brethren stood without, desiring to speak with him. Then one said unto him, Behold, thy mother and thy brethren stand without, desiring to speak with thee. But he answered and said unto him that told him, who is my mother? and who are my brethren? And he stretched forth his hand toward his disciples, and said, behold my mother and my brethren. For whosoever shall do the will of my Father which is

in heaven, the same is my brother, and sister, and mother (Matt. 12:46-50).

And in the 19th chapter of John, verses 25–27, we read:

> Now there stood by the cross of Jesus his mother, and his mother's sister, Mary the wife of Cleophas, and Mary Magdalene. When Jesus saw his mother, and the disciple standing by, whom he loved, he saith unto his mother, Woman, behold thy son! Then saith he to the disciple, Behold thy mother! And from that hour that disciple took her unto his own home.

Of course, it is generally believed that this occasion merely meant that Jesus loved and had compassion for his mother. No doubt this is true. But the greater perception of this episode reveals Jesus' awareness of his eternal birthless and deathless Nature. Therefore, again and again throughout this book, we are going to return to the absolute Fact that birth is a complete fallacy. Please be assured that once we are completely free from the deception called birth, we will be free indeed. We will be completely free, totally free, from all our seeming troubles, whether they appear to be bodily troubles or so-called problems of any nature. Yes, we will be *consciously* free from the deception called lack, or insufficiency.

Chapter VIII

Perceiving from Principle

Often, when a problem seems to confront us, we tend to consider the supposed problem first, then the one who appears to be experiencing the problem, and at last we begin to contemplate from the standpoint of Actuality, God, Principle, Infinity, the Universe Itself. With most of us, this is a sort of holdover from our background in metaphysics. But it is not the way of the Ultimate "seeing."

It is futile to attempt to contemplate the Truth *about* anything, and it is particularly useless to attempt to contemplate the Truth about nothing. The only Truth about nothing is *nothing*. Thus, we may ask, "What should be our approach when it seems that we are presented with a problem?" Most of us have realized the necessity of instant perception from the standpoint of not only seeing but *being* the universal Infinity, God, Itself. But let us now explore this subject a little further.

In perceiving from the standpoint of Infinite God, the Universe, we never consider this Infinitude as though It were something outside of, or other than, the infinite I AM that we are. It is not as though we were knowing some Truth *about* the Universe. Rather, it is an awareness of *being* the very Substance and Activity that is this Universe, God. In other words, it is perceiving from the I AM standpoint. Always we perceive from the realization of *being* that which we "see" or perceive. Thus, perceiving from the standpoint of the Infinite All, we realize that we *are* this Infinity that we are perceiving. Infinitude is the I AM that we *are* and, of course, that *everyone is.* Therefore, we find our Self-saying:

> I am the infinite, omnipotent Principle Itself. Boundless is the I AM Love, Life, Consciousness, Intelligence, Principle that I am.

Of course, it naturally follows that we realize that we are not a personalized aspect or attribute of this Principle.

The boundless, universal Principle that we are is the sum total of every Truth—every Fact—that comprises Its indivisible Eternality, Immutability, Omnipresence, Omnipotence, Constancy, Life, Mind (Intelligence), Love, Consciousness, Perfection, Beauty—*All, All, All!* Yes, every eternal, infinite Fact, all Truth, is what we are and *all that we are.* Here and now, we are the sum total of all Perfection. Being every Truth, the sum total that is all Truth, we are the complete Principle. So we can truthfully say:

> I am infinite Principle; I am the eternal, constant Omniaction—all Activity—all that is active. I am immutable Omniaction, constantly, eternally fulfilling Its purpose by being the *I* that I am.

Nothing can possibly exist but Principle. There is no Principle in assumed illusion—nothingness. Everything that exists, exists as Something. Principle is Absolute Perfection. Thus, the "Something" that is Principle *being* has to be absolutely perfect.

We hear about Reality and unreality. Well, unreality is nonexistence. Thus, unreality is nothingness. That which does not exist cannot evidence itself. Any appearance is nothingness, or nonexistence. There can be no manifestation of nonexistence. Thus, there can be no evidence of imperfection, for imperfection is not Principle, or Absolute Perfection, Only that which exists can be evidenced, and this evidence has to be the Principle Itself—Absolute Perfection—evidencing Itself. Thus, we can *only* be the evidence of the omnipresent Principle—Absolute Perfection—that we eternally, constantly, infinitely are.

The eternal Substance in, and as, the eternal Form that I am is the changeless *Eternality* that I am, evidenced. The eternal, constant, ever-present Perfection that I am is all that has ever been, is now, or can ever be, evidenced as the ever-constant, perfect Substance in Form that I am. The Hereness, the Nowness, the newness of the *I* that I am is Principle, Absolute Perfection Itself, evidenced. The Hereness is the Omnipresence that I am. The Nowness is uninterrupted, omniactive, constant, omnipresent Omniaction Itself. Thus, Hereness is an omnipresent, omniactive Truth, or Fact, and I am this Truth.

I am every Truth *evidenced* right here and now. I am complete as this Principle. I am this Principle evidenced and nothing else, or other. I am *only* the evidence of Principle, *being* the *I* that I am.

The Principle that I am is evidenced as every iota of the Substance in Form called Body, eternally, constantly, right here, right now.

Chapter IX

Self-Conscious Eternality

Often the following question is asked: Why is it that there even *seems* to be a material body, a material tree, etc.?"

Anything that appears to be matter, solidity, or density, is just that—an appearance and nothing else. It may seem to us that we see a material body called a tree, but the supposed matter, the solidity, is not in the tree, nor is it the tree itself. Where is this mistaken view of the tree? It can only *appear* to exist in and as the so-called consciousness of the supposedly born man that we consider ourselves to be.

The tree is conscious of being what it *is*. Everything in existence consists of Consciousness. Consciousness, or awareness of being, is the *only* Substance, and the Substance that is Consciousness is *always* aware of being what It is. The tree is not conscious of being a piece of temporary, solid, dense matter. Thus, the tree knows nothing whatever of our seeming misperception of it.

There is not a pinpoint in all Infinity in which some aspect of God is not aware of being and of being just *what It is*. Every atom, every nucleus of every atom, is aware of being what it is.

But let us return to our question: "Why does there *seem* to be matter in form?" It is only because the Universe—every star, planet, and galaxy—does exist that there can (to supposedly born man) appear to be a material universe. Those stars, planets, galaxies do exist. This Earth planet does exist. If this were not true, there could be no misperception about them. As we have often stated, there could not possibly be a mistake about nothing. Even if we mistakenly seem to see the tree as matter, the actual tree—consisting of Consciousness—has to exist as what it *is*. Otherwise, there could be no mistake about it. (Of course, even the mistake about it is not genuine. There is no mind existing that is capable of being mistaken.) Nonetheless, it is only because the tree exists that there can *seem* to be a misconception about the tree.

It is only because eternal Life *is* that a temporary born life can seem to be. It is only because eternal Consciousness *is* that temporary born consciousness can appear to be. Most important of all is the Fact that it is because *we really are conscious of being conscious, and conscious of things as they are, that we can seem to be mistakenly conscious, or aware, of a world that appears to be matter*. It is because intelligence *is* that we can seem to be victimized by an assumptive, born mind.

It is only because infinite Love *is* that so-called personal love can *appear* to be. Mind is conscious, for Mind *is* Consciousness. It is only because conscious

Intelligence *is* that a supposedly born thinking or reasoning mind can seem to be. (Incidentally, it is the suppositious thinking mind that falsely believes it has to be taught or to have a teacher with a separate mind. And this supposed "other" mind—teacher—is actually considered to be a greater, more complete mind than is the so-called student or follower.)

Consciousness is ever-present Awareness. It is always complete *now*. Conscious Intelligence—all Knowledge—is always present and complete as the *only* Mind in existence. Conscious Intelligence does not have to think in order to know. (Does God have to think or to reason in order to be all Knowledge?) Conscious Mind does not have to reason and wait in order to arrive at a conclusion. On the contrary, conscious, living Intelligence always knows that which is necessary to know—right here, right now. Always we exist for the fulfillment of the infinite purpose. And conscious, living Intelligence—the Mind *we* are—is constantly aware of whatever has to be known for the fulfillment of any purpose whatever.

It is true that this conscious Intelligence is not constantly focalized as every aspect of the complete Knowledge that It is. But it is also true that this all-intelligent Consciousness—that *we* are—can be and is focalized, or focused, as any knowledge that is essential to the fulfillment of the purpose of the moment. We must distinguish between the conscious, living Mind that *is* and the supposed, conscious mind that seems to be but *is not*. We must, without effort, continue in our discrimination between the Mind (Intelligence) that *is* and the pseudo mind that is not. And this goes on until there is a constancy of awareness of being *only* the conscious, living Intelligence that *is*. Of course, this does not mean that there are two minds. On the contrary, it establishes the forever fact that *there is one Mind, Intelligence, alone, and there is no other.*

From the foregoing, you can perceive that the so-called born body can only seem to be because the eternal Body actually exists. It is a Fact. When? *Now.* Where? *Here.* How long? *Eternally.* Why? Because Body is necessary to our Completeness, our successful fulfillment of the purpose in being—our existence.

It is because Hearing *is* that so-called born ears can appear to hear. But the birthless ears *are* the hearing, even as the hearing comprises the eternal ears. Hearing is a universal, ever-present constant Truth, or Fact. Hearing is not confined to ears. Rather, the infinite Hearing is focalized as the genuine and only ears. (It is the unlimited Hearing that hears the Music of the Spheres.) And it is only because Hearing is focalized as the genuine ears that it appears there are born ears that hear. Jesus said, "Having ears, ye hear not ... ."

Of course, this same Truth is true as Vision. It is only because Vision *is* that so-called born eyes can appear to be. The genuine and *only* eye is the Vision Itself. Vision is not confined to the eyes. It is infinite, omnipresent. The infinite Vision sees everywhere, even as the infinite Hearing hears everywhere. But the genuine and *only* eyes are merely the infinite Vision focalized.

From the foregoing, you can see that no one *has* hearing; no one *has* Vision. Everyone *is* Vision. Everyone *is* Hearing. Why is this true? It is true because everyone is complete Consciousness being completely conscious. So it is apparent that the supposedly born ears, even as the supposedly born eyes, can only appear to be because hearing *is* and because seeing actually *is*.

It is only because boundless, indivisible, omnipresent Activity *is* that there can appear to be matter in action, It is only because Omniaction is an ever-present Fact, or Truth, that there can appear to be any matter in action at all. Whether this Omniaction is apparent as the activity of a plane, a car, a motor, a body, or whatever is not important. It can only seem to be matter in action because omniactive Consciousness is an eternal, constant Fact. Yes, it is because infinite Activity is focalized as that specific activity that there can seem to be matter in action.

Now, beloved One, do you ask, "But what about the functions of the Body? What about bodily activity?"

It is only because the boundless, infinite Substance is constantly active that any activity can be present as bodily activity. (Actually, the Body has no activity of Its own separate from, or other than, the infinite, indivisible, perfect Omniaction that *is*.) And it is because all Substance is in Form and all Substance is constantly in action that there can appear to be a separate body in action. (As we shall presently perceive, all Substance *is* Activity because all Substance is Consciousness in action, or conscious Omniaction. Without Omniaction, there could be no Substance.) It is only because indivisible, conscious Omniaction *is* that it can seem that a supposed, separate, born body can appear to be in action.

Yes, it is only because all Substance is in and as Form that so-called material substance can *appear* to be in form. We have to see, we have to perceive, *beyond* the material appearance of anything and actually see—*perceive*—the genuine and *only* Essence and Activity as that which does exist and as that Omniaction that is active.

Chapter X

The Body that Is

The Substance in Form that eternally exists as every Body is everlasting, constant, and immutable. This actual Substance in Form that exists as every Body has to exist, else there would be no appearance of a born body. It is only because the eternal, immutable Body exists that a seemingly born body can appear on the scene. The appearance of a born body is merely a misconception about the eternal Body that has forever—and will forever—continue to exist.

It is only a misconception, or *appearance*, of any Body that seems to be or to become imperfect, to change, to age, to deteriorate, and to die. But the actual and *only* Body knows nothing about any of these fallacious appearances. The genuine and only Body can never disappear because It *never appeared to the supposed vision of assumptive born man.* But the genuine, eternal Body remains complete, perfect, untouched, uninvaded, and immune to any apparent misrepresentation about It. There can be no representation or misrepresentation about nothing. This means that the eternal, perfect, changeless Body has to exist before It can *seem* to be misrepresented.

Nothing can ever be added to or subtracted from this eternal Body that *is*. But a seeming misconception *about* this Body can appear to completely change. However, never is it the eternal, constant, immutable Body that changes. It is true that growths, obstructions, distortions, etc., can appear in or on this body that only appears to be but *is not*. It is also true that hair, teeth, etc., can seem to disappear, or be subtracted from, this superimposed body of appearance that only appears to be but is not. But every aspect that comprises the eternal Body is as eternal and immutable as is the ever enduring, genuine Body Itself. Every aspect of the *only* Body there is here — be these aspects called hair, lungs, teeth, or whatever — is just as eternal and immutable as is the eternal, changeless, birthless, deathless Body Itself.

Bear in Mind that we do not have two bodies, one that is an eternal Body and a second one that is a temporal body. *There is but one Body*, and this one Body is the eternal, changeless Body that is right here, right now. This eternal Body is substantial. It lasts forever. It is ever enduring. It consists of indestructible, imperishable Substance, which is Consciousness, Life, Intelligence, Love.

This seeming misrepresentation of Body is not Substance. It cannot last at all because it does not exist as Substance, Form, or Activity. Its apparent substance, form, and activity can only seem to be because the genuine and *only* eternal Substance in

Form—Body—does exist. Furthermore, the misconception called a temporary, born body is only our apparently temporary way of seeing the Body. But no matter how mistaken may be our temporary picture of the Body, no false view of the Body can make the eternal Body into a temporal body.

Chapter XI

You Are the Nucleus

During our classes in Vista, given in 1966 and 1967, much was revealed pertaining to the Substance and Activity that comprise the Universe. We discussed the discovery by the physicists of the fact that the entire Universe consists of something they call atoms. We will not repeat those revelations. But we will discuss further revelations of these same Truths.

We did perceive the fact that the atom is the Universe, even as the Universe is the atom. (Of course, all of this is God.) We did realize that the nucleus at the center of the atom may be likened to the sun and that the electrons that orbit around the nucleus could be likened to the stars and planets as they orbit around the sun. All of this the physicists call energy.

The following is a statement of Absolute Truth:

> Your body is the nucleus of your universal Consciousness.

Now, let us proceed to see just how and why this is true. Recently we have coined a few new words. Among these are the words *focalized* and *centralized*. Previously we had used the expression *focal point*, but somehow the word *focalized* seems to better express the significance of that which we wish to present. For instance, the expression *focal point* seems to refer to a small point in something called space. But the word *focalized* has a connotation of the entire, boundless Universe, being indivisible yet existing as Its focalization of Itself.

The nucleus is said to be light, even as our sun is said to be light. All of us have heard and read about the Body of Light. The Body of Light is the infinite Light — God — focalized. In short, the Body is the boundless, universal Light, focalized right here and now as *this* Body. Now you can joyously say:

> I am the nucleus of the universal God, right here and now. I am the infinite I AM — God — focalized right here and now. This Body that I am is the Infinite *I* that I AM, focalized right here and now. This Body of Light is the nucleus of the infinite, eternal Substance that I am, right here and now.

Everyone is the nucleus. Jesus said, "Ye are the light." He knew — and knows — that we *are* all Light. The Bible says, "God is light, and in him there is no darkness at all." Well, the Light *is* God. And there is no darkness. Every Body is the nucleus. Every Body *is* the Light, God, focalized.

Light is Life, even as Life is Light. This Light is that which the physicists call energy. Infinite Light — Life — is focalized right here and now *as* this eternal Body of Light. Thus, *God is this Body and this Body is God focalized here, now, constantly, eternally.* This Body

75

is Light—Life—eternal. Only that which God is can this Body possibly be.

This Body is God aware of being this Body, and I am That, for there is nothing else, or other, that I can be. God is all there is of the *I* that I am. That Infinitude that I am is the Body that I am.

Chapter XII

Truth Makes No Mistakes

Sometimes it appears that we are in a quandary as to what to do, what step to take, or even what decision to make. But Mind (Intelligence) is never puzzled, never in a quandary. Infinite Intelligence is Consciousness, and Consciousness is ever-present awareness of anything it is necessary to know at any moment. Intelligent Consciousness, or conscious Intelligence, is a universal Constant. It is ever-present, for it is Omnipresence. Intelligence is *all knowledge.*

This, of course, means that conscious Intelligence is the ever-present knowledge of that which is the fulfillment of any purpose that is necessary at the moment. This purpose and the fulfillment of this purpose are simultaneous. This is true because the purpose and the fulfillment of the purpose are indivisibly *One.* The purpose and the fulfillment of purpose are the *one* intelligent Consciousness in action. And there can be no separation in supposi-tional "time" between the revelation of the purpose to be fulfilled and the fulfillment of the purpose. Hence, there can be no period in which we can be puzzled or in a quandary as to the purpose to be fulfilled or the fulfillment of this specific purpose.

Sometimes we hear someone say, "But I don't want to make a mistake." Beloved, once the meaning — the significance — of the Truths which you have just read is clearly perceived, you will never doubt the rightness of any step you take. You will realize that you are that intelligent Consciousness to whom a mistake is utterly impossible. The infinite, conscious Intelligence, which is the Universe — the Mind — that *you* are cannot know or be aware of a mistake. Nor can this infinite Intelligence make a mistake.

The following statements are terse and succinct, but they will bear much contemplation. There are no mistakes. There only *seems* to be a deviation from the Truth. Truth is immutable, invariable. It is only the observation of Truth that seems to be variable. That which appears to be the magnitude of a mistake or error depends upon the difference between the changeless Truth and the rightness or correctness of our observation of this Truth. Thus, error is not really a mistake. It only seems to be a deviation, a false or incomplete way of seeing or perceiving any Truth. Right here it is necessary to realize that the Consciousness that *is* the Truth is also the conscious Intelligence that observes or perceives this Truth.

Furthermore, whatever Truth is requisite at any moment or in any situation is already present in and as the one intelligent Consciousness to whom the specific Truth is necessary. We do not search and search for the necessary Truth pertaining to any situation. We simply effortlessly perceive that the conscious Intelligence that we are *is the very Presence of the Truth it is essential to perceive.* Thus, there is no thinking, no reasoning, no weighing in the balance by the assumptive human mind. There is no waiting for the right Truth to be perceived and manifested. *Conscious Intelligence is always instantaneous perception.* This is true because intelligent Consciousness is constantly, intelligently conscious.

Therefore, Beloved, there will be no more of this fallacy of trying to reason or to ascertain how to act or what to do in any situation. You will know, and know that you know, immediately, whatever is necessary for you to know. And always you will realize that the perception of any Truth is the manifestation of this Truth.

I, Consciousness, need nothing in order to be aware of what *I* am, all that *I* am, and *only* that which *I* am. I, Mind (Intelligence) need nothing in order to *know* what *I* am, thus, to be that infinite All-Knowledge that *I* am. I, Life, need nothing in order to be alive as the eternal, constant Life that *I* am. I, Love, need nothing in order to *be* the ever enduring, living, intelligent, conscious Love that *I* am.

Whatever Substance is here this moment is *only* that which I am conscious of being. This is true because *I*, Consciousness, am the *only* Substance present as my entire Being. Whatever is active right here and now is the living, conscious Intelligence always constantly in perfect, orderly action. I am omniactive, conscious, intelligent Consciousness in ceaseless, living, intelligent action.

How can I be other than God since God is all there is to be? How can I be separate from God, when God is all there is of me?

Chapter XIII

Contemplation Evidenced as Body

Sometimes someone will ask, "Just how do I contemplate?"

To contemplate is to consider. This means to consider things as they really are and not as we wish them to be or hope they will be. It is no effort to "consider the heavens." When we consider the "works of his hands," we do not have any objective. We are not trying to prove anything. We are not hoping for an improvement of any so-called condition or situation. We are simply considering the infinite, eternal Perfection that *is*, right here and now.

Often we seem to fall back upon the metaphysical habit of doing mental work. It appears that this old habit is very subtle and deceptive. Then, too, for those of us who were engrossed in the metaphysical atmosphere and activity, this habit of mental work appears to have become deeply ingrained. Even though we know better and we know that the Absolute Truth needs no mental work in order that It be evidenced, it seems we often unwittingly revert to the former habit of working mentally. Sometimes that which is called meditation leads us right into this mental effort. This subtle deception is why I prefer the word *contemplation*.

When we are contemplating the Absolute Perfection that *is*, we are not seeking to change this Perfection. There is simply a positive, absolute, *effortless* conviction that Perfection already *is*, right here, right now, infinitely, constantly, eternally. We do not contemplate for the fulfillment of any purpose. We are fully aware that every purpose is already eternally and constantly fulfilled, and our only necessity is to be aware of this Absolute Truth.

It sometimes seems that we are trying to make an adjustment between the divine Purpose and the so-called human purpose, between God and assumptive man. Yet the Bible states that we are to keep the Mind stayed on God. It is impossible to make any adjustment between God *and* Man. When we are completely aware of the fact that we—our infinite, boundless God-Identity—are all there is to contemplate, we realize that there really is nothing but God to consider. And we do not seek to change or to improve God, who actually *is* our infinite and *only* Being.

Sometimes we wonder why the evidence of our seeing is not instantaneous. How can this evidence be instantaneous if we are always expecting it to *become* evident? The evidence already *is*. Our only necessity is to be constantly aware of this Fact. Beloved, this ultimate awareness is an eternal Constant.

Now, the following statement is of tremendous importance:

That which we are contemplating, or considering, is the evidence itself, and we, in contemplation,
are the evidence that we seem to be seeking to see
or to experience. In short, we are the evidence of
the Truth that God is All—All is God.

It is impossible for us to be separated from the
evidence of Absolute Perfection. This is true because
we *are* Absolute Perfection evidenced, or manifested.
It is not as though God and man could co-exist. God,
being, *is* Man. Thus, Man is God, being, and Man,
being evident, is God manifesting Himself, or Itself,
as just what God is and nothing else or other. Now,
how far removed from the evidence of Perfection are
we? Oh, it is all in the Bible. As we continue in the
study and contemplation of this book, many statements of Absolute Truth will be evidenced, and we
will perceive that we *are* the evidence of that which
we seem to have been seeking.

"Ye are the temple of the living God." Yes, oh
yes. The temple is the focalization of those who are
aware of being the very presence of the Life which is
God. The Temple that *you* are is the focalization—
the evidence—of the *I* that is the infinite *I* that is
your God-Identity. This is the God I AM, being. And
we read this glorious statement in Romans 8: 16, 17:

> The Spirit Itself, beareth witness (is the evi-
> dence) with our Spirit, that we are the children of
> God. And if children, then heirs of God, and
> joint-heirs with Christ.

Now, we may ask, "How is it that to "bear witness" is to be the evidence that we are heirs of God and joint-heirs with Christ?" To witness anything is to *be* that which we witness. To see or to perceive anything is to *be* that which we perceive or see. To be that which we perceive or see is to be the evidence of that which we perceive. Thus, our very awareness, or perception, that God is the Christ and the Christ is Man means that we *are the evidence* of that which we perceive.

As you continue to study and contemplate the contents of Truth in this book, the Absolute Truth revealed herein will be ever more clear and powerful in and *as* the Consciousness that you are. But right here a fact must be stated that may, to some of you, seem startling or even absurd. But please bear with these statements for a little while, and you will discover how it is, and why it is, that they are statements of Absolute Truth: *the flesh and the Spirit are one and the same*. If we are to be the *visible* evidence of the Truth we perceive, it is necessary for us to know and to understand the foregoing important statement.

> Spirit is Substance. Substance is Consciousness. Consciousness perceives. Thus, Consciousness is aware of being that which It perceives. That which is seen is Truth. That which I see, I be.

Job said, "In my flesh shall I see God. "And in John 1:14 we read: "And the Word was made flesh and dwelt among us." Neither Jesus nor Job was speaking of a body that was invisible. Could Jesus have so beautifully fulfilled his purpose in being if he had not dwelt among us as a visible Body that appeared to be flesh? No!

We simply have to stop this thing of falsely believing that our imperfect way of seeing the Body is the Body Itself. *The temple of God, which we are, is the eternal Body of the everlasting Flesh,* and when you truly see this Body, you know that this Body is visible. It is the visible, eternal, indestructible, perfect Body, comprised of Spirit, Consciousness, God, that we actually see. We call it a born, temporary body of flesh, bones, etc., but those are only names that are given to our mistaken concepts about this Body that *is*. (Remember, we have said that Consciousness is Substance.)

Of course, we have to realize that the Body of living Flesh is not a temporary, born body of matter. Let us not be deceived. That which is called a temporary body of matter is not Substance, Form, or Activity. It is only our imperfect way of seeing the eternal Body of the ever living Flesh. But we are not compelled to see the Body imperfectly. At any moment our Vision may be completely clear—our "eyes may be opened" and we may realize that we can and do see—thus *be*—this everlasting Body of Flesh. We shall perceive that this Body consists of Life, Light, Consciousness, Substance, Mind, Intelligence, Love, Harmony, and indivisible Oneness. So you see, Spirit and Flesh are one and the same thing.

This Body of the ever living Flesh that is evidenced is the Christ-Body, or the Body of the Christ. Please do not imagine for one moment that the Body of Flesh is a born body of matter. *There is no such thing as a born body of matter.* That which is said to be matter is only a mistaken way of seeing the Substance that is Consciousness, Spirit, Light, Life Itself.

Do you wonder why I keep returning again and again to the subject of Body? There are three reasons why I feel impelled to again and again refer to this subject. First of all, it seems that this is my fulfillment of purpose at the moment. To many of us, it *appears* that nuclear warfare threatens to destroy every Body —even the Body of every Thing upon this planet Earth. Our contemplation of the Body is not merely a consideration of the Body of Man. It also refers to the Body of every blade of grass, every tree, every bird, animal, insect, etc., that inhabits and comprises this Earth planet. So it is essential that all of us be completely aware of the genuine Nature of the Substance in Form that comprises Body.

Now, let us diverge for just a moment in order that the full scope of the power of our contemplation may be realized. Many students of the Ultimate know that the Consciousness we are when in contemplation is boundless and unlimited in Its scope. We have absolute proof that our revelations are perceived by those who are "full open" anywhere in the world or in our own beloved America. The aspect of Being called Body is of such great importance right now that it would be Love in action if you would contemplate the subject of Body, in the awareness of the fact that your revelations can be revealed as the Consciousness of anyone, anywhere.

Just realize that your revelations, going on right here, are going on everywhere throughout the world and that anyone who seems to be afraid may suddenly perceive the indestructible, imperishable, eternal Nature of the Body of the ever living Flesh.

There are two aspects of that which we shall perceive and consider pertaining to the so-called threat of nuclear warfare. First, we must know just what constitutes the Substance, the Form, and the Activity of every Body and every Thing. We must understand why every Body is indestructible. But above all, we must perceive just why It remains forever intact as the visible evidence that is Body.

It is the seeming failure or inability to know and to understand just what the Body is that appears to cause us to see It imperfectly. It is as though a distorted image of this ever alive Body of Flesh superimposes itself over the eternal, perfect Body that does exist. But as the so-called little "I" is transcended, this fallacious superimposition is dissolved, and we really see the ever living Body of Flesh. So it is only a suppositional, little false "I" or identity that apparently does not see the Body as It is. But this supposed little born "I" does disappear as we are more and more aware of being the I AM THAT I AM which we genuinely are. It is this eternal *I* that I am that does see the eternal Body of Man and the eternal Body of Everything.

Now let us perceive why it is that no nuclear attack can destroy this Body or any Body. We have said that the Body consists of Consciousness, Life, Mind, Love. And this is true. Even if there were such a thing as a destructive nuclear bomb or an atom that could be destructive, it could not destroy Consciousness, Life, Intelligence, or Love. Now, we are referring to the Body of the living Flesh, for conscious, living Intelligence *is* the Body of the ever living Flesh. This is the Body of Light, and there is nothing that can destroy living, loving, intelligent Light—Life.

It has been believed that Consciousness is invisible. This mistaken view has been held pertaining to Life, Mind, Love. But this simply is not true. The Substance that is Life, Intelligence, Consciousness, Love, is visible, and It is visible right here as the Substance in Form that is *this* Body. This is the Body of Flesh. This is the Body that Job mentioned when he said, "In my flesh shall I see God." And when John stated that the Word became flesh—visible *as* flesh—he was speaking of the visible Body that is indestructible, eternal, imperishable.

Actually, this Body of Flesh has always been visible, and throughout the ages there have been those who have seen It as It is. Today, more and more of us are seeing this eternal Body of ever living

Flesh, and we *know* that It is the genuine and only Body.

Now, since many of you can and do see this everlasting Body, is it not possible for anyone to see this eternal Body? Are not all of us one indivisible Consciousness? Are not all of us equally this Consciousness? *Of course we are.* And who or what can limit God?

Now, there is a second and exceedingly important aspect of this so-called threat of nuclear warfare that must be considered. Namely, it is the Substance and Activity of the atom itself. *There is one Substance.* This being true, the atom has to be this one indivisible Substance. Thus, the atom is not, and cannot be, an instrument of destruction to itself. Living, conscious Intelligence would never be Self-destructive. And above all, Love—the indivisible Oneness of all Substance—could never be made into an instrument of destruction. Love is the very Essence of the atom, even as Love is the Substance of our Being. Love is the Activity of the atom. But despite all appearance to the contrary, Love is the very Intelligence of those who imagine that an atom can be destructive.

There is one more Truth to be considered pertaining to the atom: an atom consists of the very same Substance which comprises our Body. This intelligent Substance—Consciousness—could not possibly be a destructive element to Itself. Such a possibility is inconceivable.

The eternal Body that consists of Mind, Intelligence, Consciousness, Life, Love, really is visible, and there is nothing that can make this everlasting, perfect Body of the living Flesh be or become invisible. What, then, if some so-called madman were to "push the button" that would supposedly release destruction to everybody? Could this everlasting Body, consisting of conscious, loving, living Intelligence, be invaded? Could this Body of ever living, eternal, constant Flesh become—or be compelled to become—invisible? No!

There is one thing, and one thing only, that can *seem* to disappear. Of course, even this cannot really disappear because that which does not exist cannot be destroyed or put out of existence! What is it, then, that can apparently disappear? Beloved, it is our mistaken, wholly fallacious way of seeing things. Yes, it is our imperfect, incomplete way of seeing the absolute, eternal, perfect Substance, which is all there is to be seen. This is the *only* thing that can seem to disappear. But this apparent, incomplete, mistaken way of seeing the Perfection that is the only Presence does disappear in the presence of the genuine and only Substance—Consciousness—that does exist.

This Absolute Truth can be found throughout our Bible. For instance, let us consider the following statements:

For we know in part, and we prophesy in part. But when that which is perfect is come, then that which is in part shall be done away ... For now we see through a glass, darkly; but then face to face: now I know in part; but then shall I know even as also I am known (1 Cor. 13:9, 10, 12).

Yes, it does *appear* that now we only partially know or see that which we are, and all that we are. But when Absolute Perfection, eternal, constant, glorious Life — Light — is known, we shall know — be consciously aware of — what we are, and *all* that we are, totally, completely.

It does seem that our incomplete seeing distorts our perception, and we supposedly "see through a glass, darkly." But it only appears that we see and experience a distorted image or picture of all Substance in Form. When we really see and experience God, when we truly perceive and *see* God — Absolute Perfection — "face to face," we shall all see that which *is*, and see it *as* it is. We shall realize that we *are* seeing our Self as God sees us. Yes, we shall perceive the absolute Fact that we see as we are seen. Thus, we are aware of being the one inseparable, infinite *I*, seeing, perceiving, and being Itself. God knowing and *being* Itself is the *only* Self there is, and this is the Self that we are.

Now, let us ask, "What is the purpose in this perception?"

It is essential that we realize right here and now that *we are the Consciousness that is aware of seeing*

Perfection perfectly. We are the Consciousness of Perfection, being the Perfection that is All. We are the Consciousness that does see the visible, eternal Body of perfect, ever living Flesh. We need not wait to see and to be what we are, and all that we are, right here and now. This is something that does not require a nuclear explosion in order that it *become* true and visible. Rather, *this is the way it is now.*

Some of us see all Substance in Form—and all Substance *is* in Form—as It genuinely is. Some of us *constantly* see all Existence as It is. *And all of us actually do know the genuine and only nature of the things that are.* This is true, even though we may not seem to realize the fact that our perception, our knowledge, is complete right here and now.

Before the conclusion of this book, we will further consider the necessity of seeing Absolute Perfection and that there is nothing existing that is not absolute, conscious Perfection being constantly, consciously perfect. Beloved, make no mistake about it—we are speaking of the eternal, perfect Body of the everlasting, living Flesh that is *your* Body right here and now. In fact, It is the Body that *you are* and are conscious of *being.*

There is one aspect of our discussion of the Body of living Flesh that we must clearly understand. When we speak of this eternal, perfect, everlasting Body of Flesh, we are not referring to a supposedly born body comprised of dense, solid matter. *There is no such body.* That which appears to be a material body is only a misconception or misrepresentation of the genuine and only Body. This imperishable, indestructible Body consists entirely of Consciousness, Intelligence, Life, Love. Yet it truly is visible.

Now we can joyously say:

> I consist of eternal, birthless, deathless Life. Right now I am conscious of seeing and *being* this indestructible, imperishable Body of ever-perfect, living Flesh. I am perfect Vision, seeing perfectly. I am conscious Perfection, seeing and *being* Perfection.
>
> Only the immutable Perfection that *is*, is visible, and I am the perfect Vision which sees this visible Perfection. All of this, and *only* this, am I, for I AM THAT I AM.

Chapter XIV

The Completeness that Is Omnipresent Truth

As we have stated before, this Universe is the sum total of every Truth. It exists as everything that is true, or a fact. Everything that is true—or a fact—exists and is equally present and equally true everywhere. Every Truth is a universal Truth. Thus, there is not even a pinpoint in the entire Universe where every Truth, or the sum total of all Truth, does not exist and is not known to be present. Any aspect of Existence has to exist everywhere in order to exist anywhere at all. And unless any aspect of Existence is equally present *everywhere*, it could have no existence *anywhere*.

Suppose there were such a thing as evil. Unless suppositional evil existed equally everywhere, it could not exist at all, anywhere. Unless supposed imperfection exists equally everywhere, it does not exist anywhere. Often we will hear someone say, "Oh, I know that I am part of God." This statement simply is not true. It is not a statement of Truth, or Fact. God does not exist as separate, isolated, unequal parts of Itself (or Himself, if you prefer). No! God exists equally inseparably as all that God *is*, everywhere. The Totality that is God exists *totally* everywhere.

Thus, there are no unequal, separate parts, or aspects, of God, the infinite, boundless All.

If one seems to be ill or in trouble, it may appear to him that he is a separate, isolated Identity with a specific problem that is strictly *his* trouble or *his* illness. Suppose it appears to someone that he is the victim of heart trouble. This assumption would have to do with activity that was apparently imperfect. Now, perfect Activity is a universal Truth. Perfect Activity is indivisible; It is present, and It is equally present constantly, everywhere. Thus, there can be no separate, isolated activity. Neither can there be a separate "man" who is only a *part* of this ever-present, equally present, universal Activity, which is God in action.

Therefore, because the universal, omnipresent, perfect Activity is *equally* present everywhere, there simply cannot be imperfect activity anywhere. There is no imperfect activity of anyone or anything. It is all omnipresent, equally present, God, being totally, completely, actively All.

If imperfect bodily activity could be going on, this imperfect activity would have to be equally present as *all the activity of this entire Universe*. Furthermore, all activity would be present equally everywhere. If such a horrendous thing could be, the Activity that is our entire Universe in ceaseless action would be imperfect activity. If this could be true, the Universe would be in complete chaos! Indeed, there would be no Universe at all because eons ago it would have perished. But we know that the *only* Activity that is present as this omniactive Universe is eternally, infinitely, perfect Activity. And it is true that there is no separate, isolated activity. The bodily activity is the universal Activity focalized, and it has to be as perfect as is the universal Activity. This is true because it is the entire Universe in action. There simply is no isolated, separate bodily activity because there is no isolated, separate Body.

Today we seem to be hearing much about infection. Unless infection exists equally as every nucleus, every atom, every cell, etc., it does not exist anywhere; it never has existed, nor can it ever exist. There could not be one iota of infection anywhere unless this were a totally infected Universe. By this same token, unless this is a completely perfect Universe, there is no imperfection of any kind or nature anywhere.

Most important of all, however, is the fact that the Mind (Intelligence) that knows Itself to be All that *is*, is equally present constantly, eternally, infinitely, everywhere. Indeed, it is *the Everywhere*. Therefore, unless a mind or intelligence that knows itself to be imperfect is equally present everywhere, there is no Intelligence that knows Itself to be imperfect anywhere. Unless every atom, all the Substance that is this boundless Universe, is ill, diseased, etc., there is not one iota of sick, imperfect, diseased substance anywhere.

Unless the Body of every star and planet is ill or imperfect, there is no ill or imperfect body anywhere. Not one Body, not one cell, not one so-called organ can be sick or imperfect unless this is a completely imperfect, ill universe. Unless deterioration, decay, etc., is going on equally everywhere in and as this Universe, there is no deterioration or decay going on anywhere, in or as this Universe. Unless this Universe is aging or aged, there is no old age anywhere in and as this Universe. Unless this entire Universe is constantly being born and then dying, there is nothing and no one, anywhere, that is birthing and dying.

Oh yes, we could go on indefinitely in this vein. But enough is revealed now to enable us to see, perceive, the inseparable, *equal Presence* that is God, and this All-Presence is inseparably, wholly, totally everywhere. Right now it is imperative to tell you that I have seen and known wonderful things take place through the perception of this revelation we have just been considering.

Chapter XV

God, the Universe, Is a Living, Breathing Being

The Universe really *is* Mind, or Intelligence. It is an intelligent, active Substance. The Universe really *is* conscious. It is conscious Substance. It is Consciousness *being* conscious. The Universe—God—really *is* alive. It is Life Itself being alive. This Universe really *is* Love. It is Love Itself, being loving. This Universe is a living, moving, intelligent, conscious Substance, and this living, moving, breathing, conscious, intelligent Substance is God.

This irrevocable, irrefutable fact, Beloved, reveals why it is that God really is our Life, our Mind (Intelligence), our Consciousness, and the Love we are. God is our only Substance and Activity. Thus, we are—and have to be—the Substance and Activity that is God in action. God, the boundless, universal Life lives—is *alive*—by being the Life we are. Thus, the Life we are is necessary in order that God be complete Life, or completely alive. Oh, yes, the Life that is alive as everyone and everything is necessary in order that the infinite Life that is God be infinitely, completely Life Itself. God is ever alive by being the Life that lives as everyone and everything.

Even the air itself is a living, breathing, intelligent, conscious, loving Substance. This Substance consists of something they call atoms, or atomic structures. God is Life being alive, Consciousness being conscious, Mind being intelligent, Love being loving. This *being* is the Being you are, the Being I am, that everyone and everything is, and this fact reveals just why *you really are God.* You see, *there is nothing else or other than God that you can be.*

I live, yet not "I." It is God who is alive as the Life I am. I am conscious, yet not "I." It is God who is conscious as the Consciousness I am. I am intelligent, yet not "I." It is God who is intelligent as the Intelligence I am. I am Love, yet not "I." It is God who loves as the Love I am. I breathe, yet not "I." It is God who breathes as the breathing I am. I walk, I talk, yet not "I." It is God who walks and God who speaks as the *I* that I am. I act, I move, yet not "I." It is God who acts and God who moves as the *I* that I am. I hear, yet not "I." It is God who hears as the Hearing I am. I see, yet not "I." It is God who sees as the Vision I am. I know, yet not "I." It is God who knows as the Intelligence I am. I *am*, yet not "I." It is God who *is*, as the *I* that I am. And these Truths reveal the I AM that *you are.*

Yes, I, being alive, am simply the infinite Life — God — being alive. I, being intelligent, am *only* the Mind that is Infinitude being intelligent. I, being conscious, am but the infinite, omnipresent Consciousness being conscious. I, being loving, am but just the boundless, infinite, impersonal Love, being loving. I, being perfect, am the Perfection that is God being perfect. I, being immutable, imperishable, indestructible, am only the immutability, the imperishability, the indestructible. I, being beautiful, am but the Beauty that is God being beautiful. I, being whole, complete, am only the Wholeness that is God being whole, complete, total, entire.

This fact is why "I," of myself, am nothing, know nothing, have nothing, and can be nothing.

The Only I

If I be not the Love that *is*,
I am but naught;
For Love is all that doth exist;
Tis Love not sought.
Just seeing, knowing, being Love,
I am none else.
Inseparably One. Oh, 'tis enough;
All darkness melts,
As surging, flowing, flaming Light
    is known to be
The Omni-Love beyond all blight—
    Identity.

Yes, it is all God, being *God*—but it is God, Love, Light, All, being all there is of the *I* that I am, the *I* that *you* are, that everyone and everything is. It is only in this awareness that I can even whisper, "I AM THAT I AM." The infinite, living, moving, breathing, intelligent Consciousness that I am, right here, right now, is boundless, omniactive, Omnipresence Itself. There is no other Presence.

This living, moving, breathing Consciousness that I am right now, right here, I am *everywhere*, constantly, eternally. This is true because I am unconfined, inseparable, whole, *all* Entirety, Totality. This specific focalization of the *I* that I am is the Presence that I am everywhere, constantly, eternally. Thus, the living, moving, breathing Consciousness I am is the universal Omnipresence that I am right here and now. This is the Completeness, Wholeness, Totality, Entirety, Allness I am, *being* All.

Just as God is the same everywhere, constantly, eternally, so it is that I am the same everywhere, constantly, eternally. Thus, it is not a separate "I" that is Consciousness alive here. Rather, it is the ever enduring, living Being, *being* that *I* that I am.

There is no way in which I can be a separate being because there is no way in which God can separate Itself without destroying Itself. As you can see, separation, in the final analysis, is disintegration, and to disintegrate would mean to be destroyed. God cannot, and does not, exist as separate bits and parts of the indivisible, integral All that God is. God is *one integral Whole, Wholeness, Completeness.* Hence, it is not a separate "I" that is alive here. It is the ever enduring, living, conscious Being, being the living Consciousness that I am.

Now, we know that there is nothing other than God—Infinity—here. There is no one but God alive here. There is no one other than God—Infinity—breathing here. There is no one but God acting here. There is no one other than God—Infinity—conscious of *being* here. There is no one but God seeing here. There is none other than God being seen here. There is no one other than God hearing or being heard here. There is no one but God loving here. There is none other than God experiencing here. There is no one other than God existing right here, right now, constantly, eternally.

As we know, the *only* Substance in Form here—Body—is the infinite Substance, God. (All Substance exists in and as Form.) The only Body that exists has to be ever perfect, ever enduring, immutable, eternal Substance in and as Form. This indestructible, imperishable, ever enduring Substance can never become imperfect, never age, change, disintegrate, die, or disappear.

The *only* Power here is God, Omnipotence. The *only* Intelligence here is God, the Mind that knows no trouble, sickness, lack, or pain. The only Consciousness that is conscious here is God, conscious of being. And this God-Consciousness cannot be aware of a problem of any kind or nature.

The I AM God is the *only I* here. The I AM God is the *only I* that I am. Otherwise, there could be no I, or Identity, existing here. The I AM God is the *only I* that is conscious of *being* here. If this were not true, there could be no *I*-Identity conscious of being here. The I AM God has to be the only *I* that is aware of anything or of being anything. It is only because this is true that any Identity can be aware of being, of existing, as anything or anyone at all.

The I AM Consciousness, Life, knows nothing of death. The I AM Consciousness cannot be aware of being unconscious. The I AM Mind (Intelligence) knows nothing of ignorance, or absence of Self-knowledge. The I AM Love that I am knows nothing of separated, personal love or of hatred. The I AM Perfection that I am knows nothing of imperfection. The I AM Harmony that I am knows nothing of inharmony, problems, sickness, worry, or anything that seems to be inharmonious. The I AM I that I am here and now knows only the Completeness, the inseparable, integral Entirety that I eternally, constantly *am*.

The I AM integral, conscious *Identity* that I am knows nothing of separate persons or personalities. The I AM God that I am knows no fear; the I AM God that I am knows nothing to fear. The I AM Consciousness that I am has no awareness of a suppositional human past in which there seemed to be mistakes, weaknesses, selfishness, ambition, pride, or any of the supposed human frailties. In short, the I AM God that I am, here, now, is the *only* I AM that I am, that I have ever been, or that I shall ever be.

What can the God *I* that I am know of birth? Nothing. What can the eternal God *I* that I am know of death? Nothing. Always *I* have been. Forever *I* shall be. Do *I* have any awareness of having been born? No. It is impossible for the *I* that I am to be aware of death, even as it is impossible for this *I* that I am to be aware of birth or of having been born. *I only know that I am.* What can the God *I* that I am know of being born a mortal or human being? Nothing. *I am only aware of the God I am* — Infinity, Eternality — *being.*

What can the God that I am know that God does not know and know Itself to be? Nothing. Does God, the eternal *I* that I am, know aught of birth and death — beginning and ending? No. Does the God I am — Eternal Life — know aught of a temporary life? No. Is not the God I am — Eternal Life — the *only* Substance? Yes. This being true, is it possible that I could ever be aware of a temporary substance? No. Since the God I am is the only Substance, can there be a substance that changes, deteriorates, becomes diseased, ill, or imperfect? No. The I AM God-Substance remains constantly, eternally, immutable, whole, sound, complete, indestructible, imperishable, perfect, and everlasting.

Is not the God I AM, Light? Yes. In and as this I AM God, Light, is there any darkness at all? No. Is the I AM God, Light, conscious of solidity, weight, heaviness, awkwardness, density? No.

Can the I AM God, Purity, know aught of impurity? No. The Bible clearly states that God *is of purer eyes than to behold evil.* If there were such a thing as impurity, would this not be evil? Yes. Can the God I AM Purity be aware of poison, or infection? No. Can the God I AM Purity know aught of a Substance that is, or can be, infected? No.

Can the God I AM Completeness know aught of being incomplete? No. Can the God I AM Mind (Intelligence) know aught of being incomplete knowledge? No. Can the God I AM Peace know aught of being troubled or disturbed? No. Can the God I AM Tranquility know aught of being distressed? No. Can the God I AM Order be aware of disorder? No. Can the God I AM all Supply be aware of lack or limitation? No. No. No. Can the God I AM Heaven be aware of being, or of being in, hell? No. Can the God I AM see, know, or be *anything* other than God I AM? No.

No one named Helen or John or Marie can ever say, "I am God." Only God can say, "*I* am God."

No supposed, born mortal can say, "I am God."
Only conscious Immortality can say, "*I* am God."

Chapter XVI

What Is Man?

In the Bible we read, "I will overturn, overturn, overturn it, until he comes whose right it is" (Ezek. 21:27).

Yes, it is the right, the privilege, even the necessity of the God I AM—the right and only *I*, or Identity—to reveal and to evidence Itself as the Entirety that I am. Anything that seems to be troublesome or a disturbance of any kind is simply the God I AM Identity apparently misunderstood and misrepresented.

Hell is but Heaven misunderstood, misperceived. Seeming inharmony is but the I AM God, Harmony, misunderstood. Apparent imperfection is only the I AM God, Perfection, misunderstood. The greater the so-called hell seems to be the greater is the Heaven shining through. The greater the illusion called evil *appears* to be the greater is the God, the I AM Good, shining through. The greater the supposed darkness seems to be the more brilliant is the Light shining through. The more ugly the picture seems to be the more completely beautiful is the God I AM Beauty revealing Itself. The greater the impurity appears to be the greater is the absolute Purity that is being revealed. The more imperfect the Substance appears to be the more the God I AM Perfection is asserting Itself.

The God I Am knows nothing of imperfection, inharmony, sin, evil, suffering, trouble, depravity, or impurity. This glorious God I Am knows nothing of ignorance or violence. God, the *I* that I am, knows Itself to be *only* the eternal, constant, complete harmony—Heaven, Perfection—that I eternally, constantly am. God, the I Am Omnipresence, knows Itself to be the complete answer to every supposed question. The I Am God is not aware of either the question or the questioner. God is simply aware of *being* Everything, All. Thus, God is aware of being the complete answer, all the answers to all the questions that could possibly be asked. This, Beloved, is the God I Am that *you are.*

Knowledge is God—Intelligence—knowing what God is and *all that God is.* Consciousness is God, aware of being what God knows and *all* that God knows. Life is God, being consciously alive, all that God is conscious of being. Love is God—Omni-Love—ecstatically loving all existence and joyously *being* all the total Love that Love is. All of this is God. This, of course, this means that *all of this Truth is the God I Am that you are.* This is Man. But Man is even more than all of this.

We read in the Bible that man is made in the image and likeness of God. What does this statement mean? What is an image? Does this statement mean that man is *like* God? Does it mean that man looks like God or acts like God? No! Let us examine the statement that God made man in His image and likeness.

To begin: *God did not make Man*. If God had made or created Man, then Man would have to be—or to become—something separate from and other than God Himself. Therefore, the beginning of this statement should be: "God reveals Himself—or Itself—as Man. God identifies Himself *as* Man, the eternal, constant Christ." Thus, Man cannot be separate from, *or other than*, God, and God cannot be separate from Man.

We might ask, "If God made man, where and how does supposedly *born* man come into existence? Does God make man, then permit man to destroy himself, and then remake man over and over and over again?"

Would this be God—Intelligence—in action? Would this be infinite Love in action? No! And for those who believe in reincarnation, what about this supposed man who is born and dies again and again? Does Man have the power to be either good or bad—evil—of himself, separate from God? No.

If God had made Man, we can be assured that His work would be perfect, durable, and eternal. Furthermore, this work would not have to be done over and over again. No, eternal God—Life—did not make a temporary man. But Man does exist.

God is the Christ. The Christ is Man. So God, the Christ, Man, are all One and the same. Man can no more be created than God can be created. Man *is* because God *is*. Without God, there would be no Man. Yet without Man, there would be no God. God would have no means of revealing, identifying, and evidencing Itself. Without Man, there would be no living intelligence that was conscious *of* God. Thus, there would be no living, intelligent Consciousness that was conscious *as* God. Thus, there would be no God.

Chapter XVII

Image

Now, let us explore the expression *image and likeness*. God is Omnipresence. God is the Christ, or the Christ-Man. Thus, Man is God manifested. God could not manifest Itself as an unlikeness of Itself. God could not manifest Itself as anyone or anything other than what God really is.

What is the image of God? It is noteworthy that Jesus did not say anything about being the image and likeness of God. Rather, he said, "I and my Father are one" (John 10:30). This does not sound as though he considered himself to be an image and likeness of God. But again, what is an image?

In Webster's Dictionary, the word *image* is defined as "imitation, copy, idol, a symbol." Man, the Christ, is not an imitation of God. Neither is Man, the Christ, a copy of God; nor can Man, the Christ, be a symbol for God. And in Webster, you will find the following very interesting definition of the word *idol*: "Anything that has no substance but can be seen, as a shadow or an image in a mirror." Evidently the word *image* and *idol* are synonymous. And all of us know how Moses reacted when he came down from the mountain and found the children of Israel engaged in the worship of idols.

The foregoing definition of the word *idol* should be exceedingly enlightening to those of us who are aware of the absolute Nature of all Existence. It is clear that an idol has only an imaginary substance, which is no Substance at all. But Man has Substance because Man *is* Substance. Man—the Christ—consists of the Substance which is God, the *only* Substance that exists.

The word *image* is a word coined by so-called born man. Actually, it is this same "assumptive" man who has attempted to make God in *his* image. Always the supposedly "born" man seems to have something—an image of some kind—to worship. Self-love sets up an image of itself, loves its image of itself, and even worships itself. Consequently, the only manmade image there can possibly be is this pseudo-born man's image of himself. This he also worships and calls it religion. It is this fallacious misconception of worship that he calls worship of God. Actually, it is only assumptive man's worship of himself.

Now, let us perceive, from the God-standpoint, just what this word *image* means. All there is of man is his image, or concept, of himself. Of course, man's *only* true image of himself has to be his perception of what God is. Thus, *the only true image of himself man can perceive and manifest is the way he sees and knows God to be.* Nonetheless, whatever man imagines, or images himself to be, is actually the way he *seems* to be.

Jesus was—and is—well aware of this fact. You will recall that he said, "According to your belief shall it be unto you." In order to have faith, one must believe. Thus, actual belief and faith are synonymous. In short, Jesus could just as well have said, "According to your belief, whatever you image or imagine will be, as far as you are concerned."

Yes, whatever we believe—or imagine—our Self to be is exactly the way we are going to appear to be. But this is not all; whatever we believe or imagine *anyone* or *anything* to be is the way it is going to seem to be, as far as we are concerned.

For instance, if we look at a tree and accept and believe the appearance of a temporal, material tree, this tree is going to *appear* to be temporal, material, and subject to disease, imperfection, and ultimate death. You see, if we mistake the appearance of the tree and imagine the appearance to be the genuine, eternal tree, we are going to imagine that the tree begins as the seed and thus has beginning. Hence, we are going to believe—or imagine—that the tree must deteriorate, age, and die, or end.

So long as we imagine or believe that the fallacious appearance of the tree *is* the tree, we can be assured that we have not really seen the tree at all. *A false image of tree can never be the genuine and only tree itself.* But once we clearly perceive that the image, or appearance, of the tree is only a false image—or idol—without substance, form, or activity, we are never again deceived as to the genuine

Substance, Form, and Activity that comprise all there is of the tree. Thus, we know that it is possible to actually *see* the tree as it is, rather than seeming to see it as a false image that appears to conceal the genuine and *only* tree. And Beloved, when we really do see this tree as it is, we clearly perceive that the leaves, trunk, branches, etc., are as eternal and constantly perfect as is the tree itself. *Not one leaf of the tree ever withers, dies, and falls from the tree. Genuine, illumined perception reveals the ever complete, eternal tree as the only tree present.* No longer can we be misled by any false image—or imagining—about this tree.

However, there is another aspect of this tree that is of vital importance. If we seem to see or imagine the Substance in Form that is this tree to be a substance in form that is separate from, or other than the universal All-Substance—God—we are not really seeing the tree at all. Rather, we are only apparently seeing our own false image of the tree.

Of course, we have spoken of the tree as one specific aspect of being the Infinite All, but this same Truth is true as everything we see or even imagine that we see. There is not even one Body—Substance in Form—that is separate from, or other than, the infinite, constant, omnipresent, indivisible All—God. Beloved, even if the walls of your room or house *appear* to be solid and to separate you from the infinite, omnipresent Substance, you can be sure that this appearance is not at all the genuine Substance of the walls. *There are no solid objects that can confine the Substance in Form or separate this universal Substance into particles. The mistake is only in the way we misperceive.* You will recall that Jesus suddenly appeared in the room with the disciples, even though the doors and windows were all closed.

If Man entertains an image of himself as being a *born* man, with a separate born body, man will seem to be subject to all the so-called laws that are imagined or believed to govern a supposedly born man with a born body. If Man believes—imagines, images—himself to be a sick man, an aging man, an old man, etc., this false image of man is exactly the way he is going to *appear* to be. But this imaginary kind of man is only an image—idol—and really has no Substance, Form, or Activity. This false picture is only the way man seems to believe, to see, and to image himself to be. But the genuine and *only* Man is not deceived. He is never mistaken. *He does not believe, accept, or see false images of himself.*

> Certain it is that this eternal Identity—Man— is not subject to any of the fallacious laws of supposedly born man.

Now, let us discuss this genuine and only Man. The statement that man is "the image and likeness of God" can be understood and accepted in one way, and one way only. That which follows will reveal the genuine and only significance of the foregoing statement from Genesis.

Man is God "seeing" or perceiving Himself (or Itself, if you prefer). God imaging Himself is God aware of being just what God *is*. Yet God perceiving — imaging — Himself as the Christ is Man. God's awareness of *being* what God *is*, is all Substance in Form. In this particular absolute revelation, we can perceive that Man is the image and likeness of God. Man is simply God imaging Himself as just what God knows Himself to be as the Christ, or Man.

So now let us perceive just how — in just what particular way — this fact is true as far as we are concerned. Right at this point, it is imperative that we remind ourselves of one absolute Fact: *God did not make Man*. Thus, *Man is not a created being*. Creation signifies beginning, and there is no beginning. Just as surely as there could be beginning, there would also have to be an ending. But right here and now we are to perceive just why it is impossible that God could create Man or anything else.

Again, let us say: *God is not a creator — God simply is*. And only because God is *All* being *All* can Man exist. God being Man is Man being. It is impossible for Man to be — to exist — as anything separate from, or other than, God. Thus, if Man ever began, God Itself would have to have begun or have to have begun to exist. If this impossibility could be true, God Itself would have had to be created. We have said that if Man were created — if he had begun — he would also have to end or die. In like manner, if

God ever began, were created, God would also have to end or die.

Such a ridiculous fallacy is utterly inconceivable. Nonetheless, we would have to accept this fallacy if we were to believe that God created Man. You see, whatever God is, Man is, and *has* to be. This is true because there is no other being that Man can be other than God being. Whatever is true of, or *as*, God is true of, and *as*, Man. That which God is being, God is being *as* Man. That which Man is being, Man is being *as* God.

Whatever God experiences, Man has to experience. Whatever God does not experience, and does not experience *being*, Man cannot experience or experience being. In like manner, whatever Man experiences, God has to experience. Whatever Man experiences being, God has to experience being. This is true because Man is God experiencing being Man. And God is Man experiencing being God.

Beloved, now it is clear:

> Every experience is a God-experience, and unless it is God experiencing being God, it is not an experience at all. In fact, it is a false image, or nothing, imaging itself as its own experience.

The so-called human—born man—experience is as non-existent as the so-called experiencer, which is the assumptive born man. If Man experiences birth and death, God would have to experience birth and death. And *only* if God experienced birth and death could Man experience them. In like manner, if Man experiences imperfection, disease, trouble, age, etc., God would have to experience these same inharmonious conditions. And *only* if God experienced these horrendous conditions could Man possibly experience them.

Now, why are the foregoing statements absolutely true? They are true because they are the Absolute Truth.

> God is All. All is God. God is All that exists. All that exists is God. Oh, how great, how glorious, is the Light.

Those who attended our class in Vista know that the Truths stated in the foregoing six paragraphs were not revealed during this class. But as they have just been revealed, it was imperative to present them. As the words are heard, they are written. *The hearing and the writing are simultaneous,* and oh, it is glorious indeed. And now that this wonderful revelatory experience is recorded, let us return to the text and see what is to be revealed.

Man, the image and likeness of God, seeing, knowing, and being Himself (or Itself) as God, is God knowing what God *is.* Man is simply God seeing, being, and knowing Himself to be what He—the God I Am—actually is. In this way, we can perceive that *we are the image and likeness of just what we know ourself to be.* This Self-perception is identically the same as the Self-perception that is God perceiving and being that which God knows Himself to be. Let us realize we are the very Presence of God and none other. We are this God-Presence, seeing and being just what God is, thus, what we are.

Let us image ourselves as being Perfection imaged, even as God's image of Himself is the Perfection that God *is*, imaged. It is all God, imaging the Totality that is God. Let our image of our Self be the eternal, constant Life, the immutable, perfect Substance in Form and Activity. Let our image of our Self be beginningless, changeless, endless, living, conscious, loving Mind (Intelligence) imaged.

Again, we must realize that we do not visualize ourselves as something we want to see or hope to be. It is always the pseudo-born man who tries to visualize. But we know what we are, and we simply consider the actual way we are and the way everyone and everything actually is. We know better than to attempt to draw imaginary pictures of our Self.

We do contemplate, perceive, and manifest the birthless, ageless, changeless, perfect Christ-Man that we are. We know that this Christ-Man that we are perceives that which He *is* and *All* that He genuinely *is*. This Christ-Man we know ourselves to be is the God I am, here and now, constantly, infinitely, eternally. The Christ-Man knows this Fact to be true because He is well aware of the Truth that there is none other that He can possibly see or be but God.

The God I am sees only the image of the God I am, Self-evidenced. The image is the Self-perception evidenced as the perfect, pure, whole God that I am. Because the image *is* the *I* that I am, imaging the Life, Intelligence, Love, Consciousness—Spirit—that I am, I can only see and *be* the perfect image of the everlasting, perfect *I* that I am. I can only know myself to be the perfect image of the perfect *I* that I am. I can only be conscious of being the perfect image, manifested of the perfect *I* that I am. I can only experience being the perfect image—evidence— of the constant, eternal, perfect *I* that I am.

Now, it has been said that the manifestation, the evidence, that is the genuine image is actually the I AM Substance, Form, and Activity that is God. The image is the evidence of the God I AM. This means that the image is the *I* that I am, evidenced.

The manifestation, or evidence, of the God that I am consists of the very Substance that is the God *I* that I am. The manifestation, evidence, of the Form that I am is the God *I* that I am, in Form. The manifestation, image, of the Activity I am is the omniactive God *I* that I am, in constant, perfect action.

The manifestation, the evidence, the image, has to be perfect, for the God that I am *is* Perfection. The manifestation, image, has to be eternal, for the God that I am is Eternality. The image, evidence, has to be immutable, for the God *I* that I am is Immutability. The image, evidence, has to be beautiful, for the God *I* that I am is Beauty. The image, manifestation, has to be indestructible, for the God *I* that I am is Indestructibility. The image, evidence, Substance in Form, has to be imperishable, for the *I* that I am is Imperishability. The image, evidence, has to be constant, uninterrupted, for the God *I* that I am is Constancy.

Thus, the evidence of the God *I* that I am is the very Presence of all that comprises the God *I* that I am. The evidence of this Fact remains forever intact. And this Fact is true, no matter how many false images, or idols, may seem to be produced to dispute this Truth. All the idols put together by supposedly born man can never change, delete, or alter one iota this changeless, perfect, eternal Image, evidence, of the God *I* that I am.

No falsehood can compel the Absolute Truth— God-Being—that I am to be or to become untrue. No ignorance, seeming Self-deception, can compel the eternal, constant Life I am to be or to become a temporary, incomplete born life. No falsehood or lie can make the eternal, immutable Mind (Intelligence) I am know *anything* of a mutable or changing mind, intelligence, life, love, or consciousness. No lie can compel the Consciousness I am to be conscious of— or *as*—anything that I know not and that I am not. This, Beloved, is the God I AM that you are, that I am, that everyone is.

Yes, our Consciousness that we exist is our own— and only—Substance, Form, and Activity. Everything that we see, hear, know, or experience is simply our own Consciousness, our own awareness that we exist, imaged, or evidenced. From this fact, it is clear that our own images of everything we see, perceive, or experience, consist of our own perfect awareness that we exist. Finally, we are constantly aware of the fact that our every awareness that we exist is our *only* Substance, Form, or Activity. And God is all of this. Thus, all of this is God.

The only Body we have—or are—is our own Consciousness of being, imaged. Whatever we know our Self to be is imaged as this Body. Since we are aware of the Fact that we can *only* be conscious as the ever-constant Perfection that is God being conscious, we also perceive that we can only be conscious as Absolute Perfection. We can be conscious of only Perfection because we actually *are* conscious Perfection being consciously perfect. Thus, our *only* images, or image, of our Self would have to be Perfection imaged, or perfect images.

Conscious of *being* Eternality, this eternal Consciousness of being is focalized, or imaged, as this eternal Body. Aware of being Immutability, this awareness of being is focalized, imaged, as this immutable Body. Aware of being constant, perfect Omniaction, this awareness of being is imaged, or focalized, as our ever-present bodily activity. Conscious of being Absolute Perfection, our awareness of being is imaged as absolutely perfect Substance, Form, and Activity.

Yes, our Body consists of our awareness of being, focalized or imaged. Thus, we can see that this Body is not our Body in any possessive sense. It really is the Consciousness of being that we are, conscious of being All that we are, focalized or imaged. So in a sense, instead of speaking of "my" Body, it is more accurate to say, "The Body I am."

Chapter XVIII

Loyalty versus Disloyalty

Again and again, we have stressed the fact that in the Ultimate there can be no leader and no teacher. Now let us go further in our consideration of this fact. Let us perceive just why it is of the utmost importance that we fully realize the fallacy of being followers, or even students, of *any* teacher, leader, etc.

Most of us are fully aware of the fact that to consider ourselves to be followers of any leader or students of any teacher means to limit our own Completeness. It means to deny that we are the "fullness of the Godhead bodily." We also know that for anyone to consider himself or herself to be a leader or teacher means to limit the ones that we consider to be our students or our followers. But there is more to be revealed on this subject.

I sincerely hope that I shall never hear it reported that anyone has said, "I am a student of Marie Watts," or, "I am a loyal follower of Marie Watts and her writings." So long as anyone considers himself or herself to be a follower or a student of any individual, this one is going to *personalize* the leader or teacher. Actually, there are many sincere students of Truth who firmly believe that they have found their master or their teacher. And of course, there are those who keep searching and searching, convinced that they must find the leader, Master, or teacher who is right for them.

If there could be a mistake, this really would be a most tragic one; this illusory belief is as archaic as is the worship of idols as reported in the Bible. You see, it is the fallacy of the necessity to get something from someone that seems to defeat their whole purpose in so sincerely seeking the Absolute Truth. It is this same misconception that makes it appear that there is someone outside of, and thus separate from, their own Consciousness and that this one knows more, and is more, the God-Consciousness than they are. This is futile for the student of the Absolute Ultimate. It is extremely dualistic. It is separateness, otherness.

> There is but one Consciousness, and this Consciousness is complete as each and every one of us.

The foregoing statement reveals itself as Absolute Truth.

Again and again, we have stated that each and every one of us is the Completeness, the Allness, that is God, Consciousness, being completely conscious. Our Bible says that God is no respecter of persons. It also states that the rain falls on the just and the unjust alike. Yes, Consciousness is *equally* conscious as every Christ-Man in existence. Let us not deny this glorious Consciousness, this absolute Fact, by imagining that anyone is any more God than we are. *We can never become any more of God than we are right now.*

An understanding of the foregoing statements reveals just why it is so wrong for any one of us to consider himself or herself to be a student or a follower of any so-called teacher, leader, or master. But it is equally false and tragic—perhaps more so— for the one who considers himself or herself to be a teacher, a leader, or a master. It would seem that anyone who was sufficiently enlightened to supposedly teach or to be a leader would surely know *the Allness, the ever-equal Presence of this Allness that is God being equally All, All being equally God.* Nonetheless, it appears that this fallacy continues to be present and to operate as the so-called mind of man. The so-called teacher, leader, or master always limits the ones whom he or she considers to be *his* students or *his* followers.

Invariably, the students of teachers and the followers of leaders will drop away. Never are they completely satisfied with being students of teachers or followers of leaders. Inherently they know that this attitude is wrong; that it is limiting and that it is bondage. They will continue to seek and seek, hoping to find another and higher teacher or a more enlightened leader. Always they will be disappointed. This is true because not until they discover that *they are their own revelator and their own revelation* will they have discovered the Completeness that is their own being.

It also seems to happen that the leader, the teacher, or the master will no longer appear to be visible. When this so-called transition takes place, the students or followers seem to be utterly lost. They wander around as though they were incomplete and as though never could they be any more enlightened and never could they hope to find another perfect leader or teacher. Actually, of course, they are still seeking a person to take the place of the "person" whom they believed to be their teacher or their leader. But let us ask, "Why should these so-called students or followers *seem* to be so lost?"

This appears to take place because they — the students or followers — have been trying to personalize this completely impersonal Absolute Truth. They have mistakenly believed that just one visible identity was the *only* one who could possibly speak or write the words that are revealed as this Absolute Truth. A sad corollary of this attitude is that if they read any writings other than those of their so-called teacher, if they attend any classes or lectures other than those given by their teacher or leader, they seem to have a feeling of guilt. This false sense of guilt appears to act as an obstruction to their perception of that which they read or hear. Thus, they seem to build up a resistance to the very Truth they are seeking and so earnestly wishing to understand.

Right here it is imperative that we are completely clear on one point: there is no one here named Marie Watts who is a teacher. Thus, there are no students of the one called Marie Watts. There is no self-appointed leader here, so there cannot be even one limited follower here. The writings of the Ultimate are not the writings of a pseudo person. And certain it is that no one should be—or is—loyal to an assumptive person named Marie Watts.

Loyalty is an Absolute Truth. Loyalty is a universal Constant. Yet the word *loyalty* can be misleading. You see, it has a connotation of being loyal to some separate person or some particular way of seeing or being other than the one infinite, indivisible I AM Self. It is as though there were a separate consciousness existing as a *personal* identity from whom another separate personal identity could obtain some Truth.

Loyalty to anyone other than the infinite God I—or Identity—is a false sense of loyalty. The only loyalty that is really Absolute Truth in action is loyalty, or faithfulness, in being the Absolute Truth that you are. Every acceptance of duality is disloyalty. Of course, I do not mean that merely to read some dualistic writings or to attend some dualistic lectures or classes is disloyalty. (Actually, it is almost impossible to read any writings or to attend any classes or lectures given by those along this way and not encounter some duality.) But the acceptance of duality as though it were true is disloyalty. It is unfaithfulness to the Absolute Oneness that you are. Consequently, this would mean to be disloyal to God, the Allness that is your very Existence.

127

Therefore, genuine loyalty means to be loyal, or faithful, to the Absolute Ultimate Truth. The Absolute Ultimate Truth is what you are and *all* that you are. This is the God I AM, or God being *I*, that you are. Of course, you know that when I mention the Absolute Ultimate, I am not referring merely to these writings as ultimate. *The Absolute Ultimate Truth is the complete, total Truth, no matter where you read It or hear It.* It is this Absolute Ultimate Truth that you are that requires your loyalty, your faithfulness. Someone has said, "To thine own self be true," and this is a wonderful statement.

Now, you can see that in being loyal to the Absolute Ultimate Truth, you are not being loyal to a leader, a teacher, or an author. Neither are you being loyal to a way or a path that some specific so-called *personal* identity has presented. Certain it is that no one should feel that he must be loyal only to *Ultimate Truth* writings If there were any little inconsequential "person" named Marie Watts here, I can assure you that she would be utterly incapable of writing these Truths. *Only the impersonal, infinite, indivisible God I AM Consciousness that is all Truth could reveal Itself as this Absolute Ultimate Truth.*

Sometimes when the foregoing facts have been stated, someone will say, "Yes, I know, but you are a channel for this Truth." No one is a channel for the Truth. Absolutely no one has a little, separate, personal pipeline *to* God, Who is all Truth.

Jesus knew exactly what he meant when he stated, "I am the Truth." In this statement, he really presented the fact that *every Identity is the Truth*. This is a fact because every Man is God being the Christ. It matters not that few there are who seem to be aware of this fact—it is absolutely *true*. No one can actually *be* this Truth and also be a channel *for* this Truth. But it is essential to realize that the Christ—Truth—is indivisible and completely impersonal.

To perceive this Absolute Truth is of the utmost importance for all of us. There is no such thing as Truth *and* a channel for Truth; such a thing is impossible, for Truth is Oneness and not twoness, or dualism. *There is One alone being God*. There simply is no person knowing anything, doing anything, or being anything. If this were not true, the Truth that is revealed as the completely impersonal God I AM and as the God *you are* could never be spoken or written here.

The foregoing statements do not mean that it is right to plagiarize. To plagiarize is to steal, and to steal is dishonest. Dishonesty is always the very opposite—if opposite there could be—of Truth Itself. Of course, this does not mean that anything could be stolen from a so-called person named Mary, John, Marie, or whatever. Actually, the one who descends to this dishonesty is robbing himself or herself. It seems to rob the plagiarist of his own revelations. It is true that every Identity *is* every Truth that could be written or spoken. But this Truth must and does reveal Itself in Its own specific words, or expression of Itself, as each one of us. There is an infinite variety of words and terms of expression in which this Truth reveals Itself, and when Truth does reveal Itself as Itself, It reveals Itself in Its own modes, words, or expressions. Thus, it cannot be Truth revealed if it is only a copy of words and expressions that are already revealed and expressed.

Now, it would seem that we have wandered far afield, but you will perceive that the continuity of that which is being revealed is not broken or interrupted. However, before we go on to the next subject, there is one important fact that must be stated. You will recall that I spoke of the tragic mistake it is to consider ourselves to be students or followers, teachers, leaders, or masters. In order that we may not experience any regret or any false sense of self-recrimination, the following must be realized.

In our early exploration of Truth, virtually every one of us has considered himself or herself to be a student of some specific teacher or teachers or of some specific author's writings. Some of us have almost deified certain teachers and authors. A few of us have made the mistake of considering ourselves to be followers of certain leaders or teachers. Needless to say, we were still enmeshed in dualism. So long as this seemed to be the case, our acceptance of false idols was understandable. It was only where we appeared to be at the moment. But not one of us who had reached the Absolute Ultimate was completely satisfied with this dualistic approach. Had we been satisfied, we should have searched no further than the duality that satisfied us.

But the Absolute Ultimate is Self-discovery, or the Self-revealed *to* Itself *as* Itself. Once we have perceived this significant Truth, our entire approach is one of *Self-revelation*. We know that we are the revelation and we are the revelator. Thus, we know that there can be no teacher, no student, no leader, and no follower. Once we are absolutely certain of this fact, it matters not what books we read or what classes or lectures we attend. Always we will find ourselves sifting the chaff from the wheat. Dualistic statements — whether written or spoken — will mean nothing as far as we are concerned. But any Absolute Truth we read or hear will stand out and be crystal clear. *No one can reveal our Self to our Self.* Actually, there is no other self that can reveal anything.

Now, a few more words on this subject, in order that you may realize that our Bible verifies the fact that ultimately there shall be no teachers. There are many references in the Bible stating that ultimately we are to realize complete freedom from teachers, leaders, etc. I shall quote only one of these references. (However, you may, if you wish, refer to Psalms 119:102 and Job 22; also John 6:45).

Perhaps one of the most revealing statements of this fact that each Identity is his own revelation, his own revelator, is found in Jeremiah 31:33-34:

> After those days, saith the Lord, I will put
> my law in their inward parts, and write it in their
> hearts; and will be their God, and they shall be
> my people. And they shall teach no more every
> man his neighbor, and every man his brother,
> saying, Know the Lord: for they shall all know
> me, from the least of them unto the greatest of
> them, saith the Lord.

You know that Jesus said, "I and my Father are one." Now, let us consider Jeremiah's statement of Truth from the standpoint of Jesus' positive statement of Being. In this correlation and consideration, we clearly perceive the genuine significance of the following section of the statement from Jeremiah: "they shall all know me, from the least of them unto the greatest of them." We know that the "me" in this statement refers to God, *the only Identity that is ever identified*. We are to know this God I AM and to know that this I AM is complete, entire, as all there is of the *I* that any One of us is.

We are to know that God, being the *only* Mind, Intelligence, is manifested as the *only* Mind, Intelligence, that we are. The conscious, living Intelligence that we are is complete—*All*—Knowledge. Therefore, it is imperative that this complete Knowledge be evidenced as the infinite I AM Consciousness that we are. But it is also true that the I AM that we are is consciously aware of being the I AM that is God. And of course, it is exceedingly clear that this Self-revelation will not be experienced so long as we continue to seek for teachers and leaders to reveal to us that Allness, that Isness—*that infinite Being which we already know and which we already are.*

Chapter XIX

The Total Complete Entirety
that You Are

Now, let us (at least appear to) ascend a little higher in our absolute Perception. Do you believe that you can touch something only with your hand, your feet, your Body? Do you believe that you can see something only with, or through, something which is called born eyes? Does it seem to you that you can only hear with, or through, born ears? Do you believe that you can taste something only with the mouth or smell something only with a nose?

If so, you are—or falsely believe that you are—imprisoned, encased, confined within a supposedly temporary born body. Of course, such a situation is utterly impossible. Seeing, hearing, touching, tasting, smelling are all Consciousness aware of being, and Consciousness is aware of being *All that It is*—constantly, eternally, *everywhere*. The conscious, living Mind (Intelligence) that you are is everywhere. In fact, this Consciousness is *the* Everywhere. Wherever you are, you touch, but that which you touch is not something outside of, or other than, your own Consciousness, or the Consciousness that you are. You see, you hear, you smell, and you taste, but all of this goes on as the living Consciousness that you are. Could you see, hear, touch, smell, or taste if you were not conscious? Could any activities go on if you were not alive?

Can the unconfined Consciousness be incomplete? Can the boundless, omnipresent Consciousness that you are be absent or even partially absent from Itself? Do you know nothing other than the substance and activity of this supposedly born body? Are you alive and conscious only as this which appears to be a born body? Can you not be aware of the tree, the sky, the ocean, the desert, the mountains, even though you do not seem to see them through suppositional born eyes? Can you not hear the music, the song, the symphony, even though the so-called born ear may not be listening to the singer or to the orchestra?

Can you separate the Consciousness that sees and hears from the Life that lives? It would not be possible for you to hear or to see *anything* if you were not alive, and *there is nothing alive but Life Itself.* Since you are infinite, omnipresent Consciousness, and since there is no unconscious life, you are *consciously* alive everywhere.

Are you any more conscious, are you any more alive, as the Substance of this Body than you are consciously alive as the Substance of the cloud, the sun, the stars? Are you any more consciously alive as the Substance of the Body than you are consciously alive as the Substance of the ocean, the mountain, the desert, the tree, or the grass? No! No! No! But if it *seems* to you that the living Consciousness you are is confined within a body, you will also appear to be in prison, or bound by so-called dimensions of that which you call your body. Such a thing is impossible, of course, but it can certainly appear to be genuine.

Can *any* focal point, or focalization, of the infinite, omnipresent Consciousness you are be any more or any less conscious? Can *any* focalization of the infinite, omnipresent Consciousness you are be any more or any less consciously alive? Can *any* focalization of the complete, perfect Vision you are be any more or any less Vision? Again we say No! No! No!

Chapter XX

Nothing Disappears

This body is but an infinitesimal "dot" of the infinite Body you are. Nonetheless, right where this apparent "dot" seems to be, the fullness, the Completeness that is the infinite Body, *is*. This is why the omniactive Substance that is right here, right now, is eternal, constant, and immutable. This Substance in Form, called the Body, can never perish, nor can It vanish from the everlasting Completeness that you are. This is why there is not one so-called atom, cell, organ, or any aspect of this eternal Substance in Form that can vanish. You cannot disappear from the everlasting Completeness that you are. Constantly and eternally, you are this Completeness, Entirety, Totality.

Anything you are conscious *of*, you are conscious of *being*. This is true because the Consciousness you are is the Completeness that *is* your Being. Anything you are conscious of being, you are constantly and everlastingly conscious of being. *You are conscious of being every iota of the Substance in Form that is this eternal Body right here and now.* You are never conscious of being incomplete. Thus, you are never unconscious of being what you are and *All that you are*. You cannot be unconscious of being this ever complete, perfect, immutable Substance in Form, right here and now. Not one iota of the Completeness that is this Body can disappear from the Consciousness you are.

But this is not all. This Consciousness in Form—Body—you are right here and now can never vanish or disappear from the boundless, infinite Consciousness you are. This is true because this Body never "appeared"—was never born or created in and as universal Consciousness. That which never appeared or began can never disappear or end.

You see, the infinite, ever complete Entirety that is Completeness Itself can never become incomplete. If this Body were to vanish from the universal Consciousness you are, this infinite Consciousness you are would be incomplete. Thus, the infinite, complete Consciousness you are can never be unconscious of, or *as*, this Body right here. And of course, because you must eternally and constantly be conscious of this Body, you must eternally and constantly be conscious *as* this Body.

Now it is clear that this Body has to be as eternal, constant, and as complete as is the universal, indivisible, eternal, constant Consciousness you are. How, then, would it be possible for this Body to die, to disintegrate, and to disappear into oblivion? *It is not possible.*

There is no death. There is no body that dies. Death is impossible because the infinite, eternal

Consciousness—Substance—is the eternal, conscious Substance in Form that is this Body right here.

There are no vacuums in Omnipresence. If there were such a thing as a vacuum, this vacuum would have to consist of nothingness. If this could be true, this Universe would be literally filled with pockets of nothingness. Yes, these seeming vacuums in the omnipresent *I* that you are would mean that wherever a vacuum—or nothing—was, you would not be conscious, or conscious of being. Where, then, would that leave the infinite, omnipresent, indivisible Consciousness that you are? *Nowhere at all.*

Right here, at this focal point, there is Mind, Life, Consciousness, Love. This is the genuine and only Substance there is, here or anywhere. Yet It is apparently invisible. Apparently It cannot be seen by supposedly born eyes, yet It does exist, and It exists as *All that actually is.*

This seemingly invisible Substance is the omnipresent, conscious Mind (Intelligence) *that knows what It is,* constantly, eternally. This is "the true Light, which lighteth every man that cometh into the world" (the world of appearance or illusion). But as we have often said, the world of appearance can only *appear* to be, and it can only appear to be because the seemingly invisible Omnipresence *is.* That which appears to be present here and now is not Mind, Intelligence. It does not even know that it appears to exist. It does not know what it appears to be. Being complete darkness, "mindlessness," it cannot know one single thing of, or about, itself.

An appearance can know nothing of either pleasure or pain. It knows no sensation. It cannot know either joy or sorrow, harmony or inharmony. Being completely nonexistent, it knows nothing of Existence. It cannot know itself to be either good or bad, perfect or imperfect, young or old, painful or painless. This is true because the *only* Substance here and now that knows anything is the seemingly invisible Substance which is Mind, Intelligence, right here and now.

Sometimes we speak and hear the words *nothing* and *nothingness* so often that they become meaningless to us. Perhaps the word *nonexistence* would be more clear and potent. Most of us have spoken the words real, Reality, and unreality. During our experience in metaphysics, the word *Reality* seemed quite important to us. Nonetheless, always it seemed that the word *unreality* was just around the corner. This word really did mean something to most of us. But it had a connotation of something else, or something other, that was not Reality presenting itself. Of course, unreality was simply error, but it appeared to some of us that error itself was something or had existence. Perhaps the words *Existence* and *nonexistence* would be better. At any rate, once we are perceiving from the Absolute standpoint, we find that the words *Reality* and *unreality* are no longer present in our vocabulary. It is rarely that these words are found in the writings of the Ultimate.

That which we called *Reality* exists; thus, it should be called *Existence*. That which is called *unreality* or *unreal* does not exist; thus, we should call it *nonexistence*. That which is eternal, infinite, immutable does exist. It is Existence. That which is temporary, circumscribed separate, mutable, confined does not exist. Therefore, it is nonexistence. Any appearance of *anything* that is not eternal, infinite Perfection is only an appearance, without Substance, Form, or Activity. It is devoid of Intelligence, Life, Love, Consciousness. *It is not God.* Thus, it does not exist. Therefore, we speak of it as being nonexistence.

In order that anything exist, it has to be Existence. Nonexistence, being nowhere, cannot exist anywhere. Existence alone can manifest Itself as Substance, Form, Activity. Can nonexistence manifest itself as Existence or as something that really does exist? Can nonexistence know itself to be or to be anything? Can nonexistence manifest itself as conditions? Can this complete absence of anything be or become the presence of something?

Existence is immutable, infinite, eternal, omnipresent Perfection. This is Existence evidenced *as all that is, or can be, evidenced*. Where does this fact leave any appearance of imperfection? Right where it belongs—it leaves it without any existence at all.

Any illusion of lack is an acceptance of the fallacy that nonexistence exists. Lack would be an absence of Substance, Form, and Activity. Supply is the ever-existing Presence of Substance, Form, and Activity. Supply is Existence. Lack is nonexistence. Thus, Supply *is*; lack *is not*. Any limitation would have to be at least a partial absence of omnipresent Supply. But we know that Supply *is*. We also know that there can be no "partials." Thus, limitation is nonexistence. Infinite, omnipresent, constant Supply *is*.

Again, complete Supply *is*. It exists. It is Existence. In speaking of lack or limitation, we do not confine ourselves to that aspect of Supply called money. Eternal Life, Consciousness, Intelligence, Love are Supply. Complete Harmony, Joy, Peace, Fulfillment are Supply. Ever-perfect Substance, Form, and Activity are Supply. All that is infinite, indivisible, immutable, constant *is Supply*. All of this Supply is Existence. The absence, even for one second, of this indivisible Allness would be nonexistence.

We are *never* concerned with nonexistence. Our entire attention is devoted to Existence, or that which does exist. Any appearance of solidity, darkness, inharmony, imperfection is nonexistence. Oh, we are aware of what it *appears* to be, but we are unconcerned. We can't be bothered by anything that we know does not exist. We keep our Consciousness "stayed on God." You see, God *is* Existence. An appearance is nonexistence. It has to be this way, for *God is All—All is God.*

There can never be *any* manifestation of an absence. Neither can there be an unmanifested Presence. An absence cannot manifest itself as a presence. Only that which is present can evidence Itself or be evidenced. *God is Omnipresence*. But it is necessary to also perceive that *Omnipresence is God*. This means that *the only Substance, Form, or Activity present eternally, infinitely, constantly is God*. Again, only that which is present can be manifested. *The Presence is the Manifestation; the Manifestation is the Presence.* The Presence is Existence, and the Existence is the Presence manifested.

Suppose that some imperfection should seem to be evidenced. *God, Absolute Perfection, is the Presence.* Hence, Absolute Perfection is manifesting Itself right here and now. Imperfection would appear to be an absence of Perfection—but nonexistence, an absence, cannot manifest itself as anything.

Suppose that death seemed to be imminent. Life is the constant, eternal, infinite Presence. The Presence, Life, is all that can be manifested. Death would be an absence of omnipresent Life. As stated before, non-existence, an absence, cannot evidence itself as Presence.

Suppose that some activity, whether it be business or bodily activity, should seem to be imperfect. *Omniaction is Omnipresence; Omniaction is perfect, intelligent Activity, for Intelligence is Omnipresence.* Therefore, perfect Activity *is*; It exists and It is manifested.

Imperfect activity being nonexistent, completely absent, cannot be evidenced at all.

Suppose that Vision seems to be imperfect, incomplete, or even absent. Vision is omnipresent because Vision is Omnipresence. Vision is Completeness and Completeness is Omnipresence. Perfect, complete Vision exists. Thus, perfect, complete Vision is manifested. Imperfect, incomplete Vision is not. It is nonexistence—an absence—thus, it cannot manifest itself as a presence. This same Truth is true as Hearing. Perfect Hearing exists; thus, perfect, complete Hearing is manifesting Itself.

Suppose that the teeth, or any aspect of the Substance in Form that is the Body, appear to be deteriorating. Immutability is omnipresent because Immutability is Omnipresence. Immutability *is*; It exists; thus, Immutability is manifested. Mutability would appear to be an absence of Immutability. An absence is nonexistence. Nonexistence cannot manifest itself as though it were Existence. Nonexistence cannot evidence itself as any condition.

There are no conditions. All Substance in Form is wholly, completely unconditioned; thus, constant, eternal, infinite Being has no awareness of conditions. Eternal, constant Life is normal. Eternal, constant Perfection—complete harmony— is normal.

Awareness of being constant, perfect Activity is normal. That which God is, and *only* that which God is, is normal.

The foregoing Truths may be perceived in and as every contemplation. This is not a method. It is essential that every Truth be perceived as *your own revelation*. However, should any seeming abnormalcy, imperfection, etc., present itself, it will be most helpful to—in your own way, in your own words—perceive these Truths. You may be surprised at the further revelations you will experience and at the *glorious manifestations of these revelations.*

Chapter XXI

Why Do Problems Seem to Exist?

Now, of course, the usual questions arise. "Why should it seem that these abnormalcies, imperfections, problems, etc., even appear to be genuine? Why do they seem to be evident?"

The seeming problem is always nonexistence. It of itself is an absence. So it goes without saying that it can never be an evidence of Existence. There can never be an awareness of a problem. Thus, there can never be a manifestation of a problem. There can never be a consciousness of an absence or non-existence. Without a consciousness of a problem, there can be no problem. Hence, the seeming imperfection, or abnormalcy, simply cannot even *seem* to be genuine to and *as* the absolute, ultimate, eternal, constant Consciousness that you are. *You cannot be conscious as an awareness of nonexistence.* You cannot be conscious as an awareness of any evidence of an absence. Thus, you cannot be conscious of even a seeming abnormalcy or imperfection.

Never are you conscious of a problem or abnormalcy. In order to be aware of something that does not exist, such as a problem, you would have to *be* the problem. *It is in this same way that, if God were conscious of any imperfection, God would have to be the imperfection.* In any event, any apparent consciousness of an abnormalcy would mean that the consciousness was the nonexistent abnormalcy, the inharmony, etc., and this would mean that the Consciousness that you are was nonexistent. *Thus, You—the eternal, ever-present, complete, immutable, perfect You —would not exist.* Now, I know these last few statements will bear some study and contemplation. But I also know that *the ever-present Consciousness that you are* will be completely aware of the tremendous significance of these few statements.

Any imperfection would be incompleteness. Any imperfection would be an incomplete Consciousness, or awareness of incompleteness—a seeming awareness of not being infinite, constant Completeness Itself. *Completeness is an omnipresent, constant Truth, or Fact.*

Suppose it appears that the hair of your head is falling or disappearing. Then again, suppose the teeth appear to be deteriorating, even disappearing. It is never a deterioration of the teeth that is being revealed and manifested. A tooth that was deteriorating would have to be a tooth that was in the process of becoming incomplete. It would even seem to be in the process of destroying itself, or becoming extinct. *This is impossible. Intelligence does not destroy Itself.* A missing tooth would mean incompleteness, even as one missing hair would mean incompleteness.

The Bible says that "every hair of your head is numbered." There is never one more or one less tooth. There is never one more or one less hair. It is never a missing tooth or a missing hair that is revealed and manifested. *An absence of anything would be nonexistence.* There can be no manifestation of an absence, or an absence of Substance, Form, and Activity. That which does appear to be incomplete is *merely our apparent incomplete awareness of all Substance, Form, Activity.* Yes, it would also be a seeming incomplete awareness of the eternal, immutable Nature of all Substance in Form.

The only answer to this fallacy is that we be completely aware of *being* the complete, indivisible, omnipresent Universe Itself. Awareness—Consciousness of Being—*is all Substance, all Form, all Activity*, and the Substance, Form, and Activity have to be as eternal, as constant, and as omnipresent as is Awareness, or Consciousness of Being.

Oh, Beloved, this is why it is so absolutely essential that we consider everything from the standpoint of being boundless Infinity Itself. Our Completeness is infinite because Infinity is our Completeness. Some of us have seemed to approach this Absolute Truth from an entirely false basis. We have attempted to expand into Infinity, but all the while we *were* Infinity Itself. Some of us have begun our contemplation from the standpoint of an infinitesimal focal point. Then we have attempted to concentrate our attention at this focal point until we expanded into Infinity. *All of this has been the manipulation of a kind of mind that does not exist, attempting to inflate its own nonexistence into infinite Existence.* Never are we going to know completely what we are, and all that we are, until we constantly are aware of being the Infinite All that we are.

Our seeming incomplete awareness is why it seems that we are aware of problems, abnormalcies, etc. The only imperfection, abnormalcy, there even seems to be is that we *appear* to be incompletely conscious of the boundless Infinitude that we are. That which we are infinitely—and *All* that we are infinitely—we are specifically. It has to be this way because Infinity is Omnipresent—constantly, eternally, and immutably.

Does this mean that we are to ignore this focalization of our infinite Completeness which is our Substance and Activity right here and now? Does this mean that we are to be unaware of the focalization of our infinite Being, our daily affairs, our professions, our homes? No! No! No!

Although we are always conscious—consciously aware of being infinite—we are also conscious of being specific. It is our infinite Being, *being* specific, that is evidenced as our daily affairs, our homes, and as the entire Body. We must perceive that the focalization of our Infinitude does not mean division or separation. Our Infinitude is absolutely inseparable.

Absolute Completeness—in which not even a seeming problem appears to present itself—is the Infinite, being the specific. But this Completeness is also the specific being the Infinite. It is the infinite

Identity that you are, and it is the specific Identity that you are, being the infinite Identity that you are.

> Heaven is not something that we are going to become conscious of being. Rather, Heaven is the complete Entirety of our Being, here, now, eternally, infinitely.

It is in our complete awareness of being infinite yet specific, and specific yet infinite, that we are conscious of being what we are and all that we are.

Now, let us discuss the specific Identity that we are. We must not ignore our specific Identity. but above all, *we must be ever conscious of being the infinite Identity that we are.*

Chapter XXII

Being Specific Is Self-Identification

Self-identification is right and necessary. But we must be alert in Self-identification, or being specific. So often the very word *specific* seems to present a picture of separate material substance in form, called the body. But the specific Identity, or the infinite Identity being specific, is far more than a body. It is the complete focal point of our daily life and experience. It is our specific fulfillment of purpose in *being* focalized here. There is nothing haphazard in or as the Infinity that we are. Thus, there definitely is an infinite, but also a specific, purpose to be fulfilled by the focalization of the Identity that we specifically are.

It is true that the infinite Consciousness that we are is focalized as the Body. But it is well to realize that there is no difference between Consciousness being the Body and consciousness being *all the Substance and all the Activity that comprise our specific focalization of being.* It is only because the assumptive man's view of the Body appears to be distorted and false that the Body seems to be blocked off into a certain area of something called space and separated from the entire Substance of the Identity. *Infinite*

Consciousness remains the same, whether It is manifest as a Business or a Body.

Being specific as the Body simply means that the infinite Consciousness you are is aware of being focalized as this Form. Being specific is also being fully aware that you are eternal, constant Life, Intelligence, Consciousness, Love, and infinite Indivisibility. All of this Infinitude that you are, manifested as the Form that is this Body, remains exactly the same Substance that is your Infinitude. Every Fact that you know the infinite, omnipresent, eternal Existence to be is present and evidenced now, here, as all there is of this specific Body. In short, this Body *is* the infinite, constant, eternal Being that you are—complete, wholly, totally, as this Substance in Form that you call Body.

Again it must be said: it is wrong to entirely ignore the specific Identity. But it is also a mistake to ignore this infinite, yet specific, Identity that is manifested as this Body. To completely ignore the specific Identity you are amounts to a denial of the infinite Identity you are, manifested as this Identity right here and now. In like manner, to totally ignore this infinite, yet specific, Body you are is to deny the very presence and manifestation of the Body Itself. *Never deny the Body.* It does exist, and Its Existence is an eternal Fact.

This Body is absolutely necessary to your Completeness, and *you are Completeness Itself.* If your Perception were not focalized as this Body, this

Body would cease to be evidenced. *You cannot exist as a bodiless or formless identity.* Again, *all Substance exists in and as Form.* You are never concerned about, or for, the Body. It is well that you do not focus the attention on or as the Body. You cannot avoid being conscious *of* the Body, however, because your very Consciousness that you exist is the Substance, Form, and Activity that is the Body.

Always remember that the Body needs no help in order to be—and to remain—eternally, constantly perfect. This is true because the Body consists of infinite, eternal, indivisible, constant Perfection. And this, Beloved, is why It is and ever remains consciously perfect.

Chapter XXIII

"Get Thee behind Me, Satan"

There is tremendous significance in the above quotation of Jesus. But he also said, "Having eyes, ye see not." At first glance, it may appear that these two statements are not correlated at all, yet they are correlated. "Get thee behind me Satan" (Luke 4:8) really means "Get out of my sight; I cannot be compelled to see anything that does not exist." "Having eyes, ye see not" (see Mark 8:18) means that because we seem to see things as they are not, or as they merely appear to be, we apparently fail to see things as they *are*. Because we apparently are so busy looking at an appearance, a nonexistence, we do not actually see that which does exist. It is no wonder that Jesus said, "If ye were blind, then ye would see" (See John 9:51). Yes, if we were blind to an appearance—nonexistence—that seems to conceal Existence, we would actually see—thus, consciously be—Existence as It genuinely *is*.

"Having ears, ye hear not," said Jesus. He knew we were so busy listening to false reports—or the things of the world of appearance—that we did not hear "the still small voice" which is all that can really be heard. What is it that we really see when we see that which does exist? We see the boundless, omnipresent Consciousness that we are, in Its glorious, beautiful Form and Activity. What is it that we hear when we are really hearing? It is the Music of the Spheres. It is the Beauty that is Perfection, the Perfection that is Beauty. It is Substance, Form, and Activity. (Oh yes, you can hear Substance, Form, and Activity.) It is the "still small voice" of the Consciousness that we are. Above all, it is Music, Harmony, Perfection. It is Heaven here, now, every-where—infinitely, constantly, and eternally. *We really hear the Consciousness that we are.*

You see, seeing and hearing really mean far more than has generally been realized. It is all a matter of *Consciousness perceiving,* or conscious aware-ness of being. And just as surely as Consciousness perceives, or sees, Form and Activity, so it is that Consciousness hears Substance, Form, and Activity. The Consciousness perceiving and the Conscious-ness hearing are the same thing.

Sometimes when we seem to be ill, we really appear to focus our attention upon the supposed illness rather than upon the Perfection that really is our Substance. This is particularly true if we appear to be in pain. It is understandable that our attention should be focused in this way because that which is called pain does appear to draw our attention to the supposed area of the pain. But actually, any supposed bodily illness or inharmony can only *seem* to endure so long as it can claim our attention. Once our entire attention is involved in perceiving the Perfection that *is* rather than the seeming imperfection that *is not*, the apparent illness, pain, or whatever, no longer even *seems* to exist. But it is true that we apparently are so busy being aware of our supposed aches, pains, problems, and our seeming imperfections that we apparently are not aware of the complete Perfection, Harmony, etc., that is actually all that is here as the Entirety of our Being.

There is another aspect of this seeming blindness that should be considered. It appears that we "seek a sign" that will show us whether or not the Truth is true or whether it is working. Jesus pointed out this fallacy when he said:

> Why doth this generation seek after a sign? Verily I say unto you, There shall no sign be given unto this generation (Mark 8:12).

Yes, we do seem to "seek after a sign," namely the evidence of the Perfection we already are. The seeking is the so-called mental effort, or trying to perceive the Perfection where the apparent imperfection appears to be. This effort seems to defeat our purpose. Why? Because in *trying* to see, or to perceive, so-called human perfection, we are denying the very presence of the Perfection we hope to see evidenced. Thus we are—or appear to be—focusing our attention upon the presence of the supposed illness, pain, problem, etc., rather than upon the Presence that is God being what God *is* constantly, eternally.

The Bible presents the answer to this fallacy:

Thou wilt keep him in perfect peace, whose mind is stayed on thee: because he trusteth in thee (Isa. 26:3).

What does it mean to "keep the mind stayed" on God? It means *constancy*. It means that no matter how persistent or how insistent the apparent problem seems to be, the Consciousness we are must be the Constancy we are.

Oh, yes, we are Constancy. We have to be Constancy because Constancy is a universal, omnipresent Truth. And as often stated, we are all Truth, or the sum total of all that is true. But the significance of this entire presentation is that we are not to "seek a sign." We are not to make an effort. We are not to try to *do* something—even mentally—about it. We are not to *try* to see—perceive—the Perfection that already *is*.

Rather, we are to constantly—or as effortless Constancy Itself—be aware and *remain* aware of the Presence that is God. It is in this constant awareness of the Presence that is God that we perceive the glorious Fact that *we are this Omnipresence Itself*. Thus, we are the very presence of the Perfection we seem to have been seeking, and this awareness, Beloved, is the presence of the conscious Perfection that we are —here, now, eternally.

We pay no attention to *any* appearance. We are not busily engaged in looking at an appearance which is merely nonexistence. Nonexistence is not a cause. Neither is it an effect. Nonexistence is not Substance, Form, and Activity.

Even the astrophysicists are increasingly aware of this fact. In a recent scientific magazine, there was an article by an outstanding scientist. In substance, he stated that the Universe, as man knows it, is simply an artifact of the human imagination.

Chapter XXIV

The Genuine Significance of Judas

All of us are familiar with Judas' betrayal of Jesus, the Christ. There is great spiritual significance in this recorded episode, as reported in our Bible.

Every so-called born man is a Judas.So long as we seem to believe we were born, we are going to also seem to be a betrayer of the Christ. It is interesting to note that Jesus knew Judas was going to betray him, yet he went right on and permitted his own betrayal.

One might ask, "Why?" The answer is simple. Jesus knew the spiritual significance—the Truth— behind and beyond this entire experience. Jesus knew that Judas could not really betray him, but that the betrayer could only seem to betray himself. *Any self-deception is self-betrayal.* Someone has said, "No one and nothing ever deceives us. We can only deceive ourselves." This is true; however, even self-deception is but a "seeming." It can only *appear* to go on in the realm of the pseudo-born man. Jesus knew that no one, or other than himself, could betray him. And he also knew that he was not self-deceived.

The Absolute Truth that is signified by the apparent betrayal of Jesus is that *we are never deceived or betrayed*. As stated before, we can only seem to betray ourselves. Self-betrayal is one of the worst aspects of dualism. Any mistaken belief that there is anyone or anything other than the God-Self is Self-deception, thus, Self-betrayal. Any illusion that we can exist as anyone or anything separate from, or other than, the I AM God being All is Self-deception, or Self-betrayal. And this can only *seem* to be the Self-betrayal of the *supposed* born man. Actually, the illusion of duality is Self-deception, or Self-betrayal. Never is the God *I* that I am, that you are, betrayed. It can only seem to be the Self-betrayal of the supposed born man.

We know that actually we are God being the Christ, or the Christ being God. We are told that Judas betrayed the Christ. The so-called illusion of being a born man is the only betrayer. This supposed "man with breath in his nostrils" is the betrayer of our genuine and *only* Being — the Christ — that we are. It is as though the pseudo-born consciousness betrayed the birthless Christ-Consciousness that we truly are. But we know that the Christ we are can no more be deceived than could the Christ that was — and is — Jesus.

If there were such a thing as a deceiver or a deception, it would inevitably mean self-destruction. (You will recall Judas' apparent suicide, or self-destruction.) This apparent self-destruction is but a portrayal of the self-obliteration of any illusion or any delusion concerning Man. Any duality has to be temporary. This is true because apparent duality is nonexistence. It has no basis in Fact, or Absolute Truth.

> Absolute Truth is the *only* Truth. Duality is not Truth at all. It is not true; thus, it does not exist.

We simply cannot combine dualism and Absolute Truth. It will not work. It can only lead to confusion and frustration. This is true because one contradicts the other. *Any departure from the Absolute Truth that God is All, All is God, is Self-deception, thus Self-betrayal.* Therefore, to attempt to be both dual and Absolute must always obliterate itself. However, if the Absolute seems to be too vague or too transcendental to you, it is far better to continue on with the dualism of metaphysics. You see, metaphysics is duality—twoness, or otherness. The Absolute is complete, indivisible, infinite Oneness, and this One is God.

If we attempt to be both Absolute and dual, we apparently are trying to divide ourselves. We are trying to be two. Thus, we cannot really be anything. And our Bible clearly states: "A house divided against itself cannot stand" (Matt. 12:25). You will find many references in our Bible that reveal the futility of attempting to be both Absolute and dual. Among these references are Mark 3:24-25 and 1 Corinthians 1:10-13. Jesus did not—and does not—diverge from his constant perception of being the Absolute—*God is All, All is God.* This fact is exceedingly apparent in

The Gospel According to Thomas. Thus, Jesus could not possibly have deceived or betrayed his Christ-Self.

Jesus was completely untouched and immune to the seeming betrayal of Judas. The birthless Christ-Man is never touched by any of the seeming deceptions of a supposedly born man. The birthless Christ is Its own immunity to all duality. The Christ-Consciousness has no awareness of duality, self-deception, or self-betrayal. The Christ-Consciousness could never deceive Itself.

It really is noteworthy that Jesus — the birthless Christ-Man — was completely untouched, unaffected, by the seeming betrayal of Judas. Totally unconcerned, he went right on being Love Itself. This Love was so beautifully portrayed in the final episode at the scene of Jesus' apparent betrayal. Somehow it seems requisite to present this infinite Love in action now, right here:

> When they which were about him saw what would follow, they said unto him, Lord, shall we smite with the sword? And one of them smote the servant of the high priest, and cut off his right ear. And Jesus answered and said, Suffer ye thus far. And he touched his ear, and healed him (Luke 22: 49-51).

Beloved One, to me this episode has always been the most glorious evidence of the Christ-Love that could be manifested.

Let *us* be aware of being this Christ-Love. The birthless God being the Christ — that we are — is never touched by the seeming self-deception of supposed born man. We are completely immune to the entire seeming illusion. We just go right on being the birthless, ever living, intelligent, conscious *Love* that we *are*. Love is our immunity. Just knowing we are the Christ, and nothing else, is *being* the Christ. *It takes the Consciousness that is the Christ to know that It is the eternal, birthless Christ of God being man.*

We now perceive that the eternal God-Being—or Identity—is constantly and eternally Self-maintained and completely immune to any appearance called a temporary born man.

Chapter XXV

Some Clarifications

At this point, it is imperative that the following clarification be stated. I am well aware of the fact that the Allness, the Onliness, that is God has been stated repeatedly. It is possible that sometimes it may have seemed rather repetitious. *God is All, All is God*. This basic Truth has been stated in an infinite variety of words and combinations of words. The repetition has been—and is—necessary, as we shall now perceive.

First of all, we do have Biblical authority for the necessity of the frequent repetition of this basic Truth:

> For precept must be upon precept, precept upon precept; line upon line, line upon line; here a little, and there a little (Isa. 28:10).

Now, one may question: "Why should this constant reiteration be necessary?" This reiteration is truly imperative because the basic tendency of all of us seems to be to fluctuate between the Fact—God is All, All is God—and the fallacy that something exists that is not God. It seems that we will repeatedly reiterate the *Allness*, the *Onliness*, that is God, and then, without even being aware of a contradiction, we will find ourselves believing in a presence or a power that is something other than God.

But this is not all. Often we find that we are *acting* as though we were someone that God could never be. And as long as we continue to vacillate in this way, we are going to seem to continue to fluctuate between Perfection and imperfection, Harmony and inharmony, Completeness and incompleteness, etc. As we appear to vacillate, so will our manifestation, our evidence—of seeing and *being* just what God is—appear to vacillate or fluctuate. Constant, perfect evidence does require a Constancy of our awareness that *God is All, All is God.*

This constant awareness of the Allness, the Onliness, that is God generally does not seem to burst forth suddenly in and as our Consciousness. It does appear to be a gradual experience. Actually, of course, it is Self-revelation. But because it does appear to be revealed "here a little, there a little," as Isaiah perceived, it really is necessary to hold this glorious Absolute Truth very close indeed within and *as* the Heart. Sometimes, when it seems that we are just so busy that we almost can't maintain this awareness, it helps tremendously to just softly say "God, God, God." Just to whisper this wonderful word is all that is required to be aware of the Presence. Again and again during the day and night, I find this word *God* speaking itself—and many times repeating itself—as the Consciousness I am.

Perhaps some other word will have the same significance to you, but the one word *God* is all that is necessary as far as this Identity is concerned. I have explained why this one word *God* means so much as my experience, so I shall not repeat the explanation here. But I can tell you that just softly — and oh, so lovingly — uttering this glorious word immediately reveals the Omnipresence that is God and reveals that the entire Existence that I am is this Omnipresence.

Now, let us clarify another point that has sometimes puzzled certain students of the Ultimate. Throughout these writings, you will find many statements that sound negative. Yet we have clearly stated that we have nothing to do with affirmations and denials. It is true that often these statements refer to something that is not God, something that is not the I AM that you are, or something that does not really exist. Thus, it is not surprising that some questions should arise about these seeming contradictions. Please be assured that *these negative statements are not a denial.* Let us now perceive why it has been — and is — necessary to present them as they are revealed. (Incidentally, *only* that which is revealed is ever presented in and as the writings of the Ultimate Absolute.)

When someone calls or writes a practitioner, or consultant, for help, he has to speak in statements that appear negative. Often, even as this one is asking for help, he really feels that he is making statements that are untrue. Yet, it seems imperative that the seeming untruth be stated. *The consultant, or practitioner, does not ignore these statements.* But neither does he consider them to be statements of Fact, or of Truth. And, of course, he does not deny the untruths. Why should he deny anything that he already *knows* does not exist? How does the consultant know the nonexistence of the fallacious report? Beloved, he cannot avoid being aware of the nonexistence of any apparent inharmony because he is so fully aware of that which does exist. This is why it is so very essential that the consultant be— and remain —*a constant awareness of that which does exist*—God.

Now, we may wonder why it should be necessary to make any negative statements at all. We may also feel that no purpose is served or fulfilled by presenting the false picture to the consultant. Nothing could be further from the truth. Most definitely there is purpose to be fulfilled by these statements. Whenever any specific so-called problem appears to be present, it always means that some specific Truth is actually revealing Itself. The purpose of the revelation is in being the *evidence* of the Truth that is being revealed. Therefore, the consultant is immediately aware of the specific Truth that is being revealed, rather than of a nonexistent problem. But this is not all: the consultant is also aware of the certain Fact, or Truth, that he, as well as the one who called for help, *is the very presence of the specific Truth that is being revealed.*

In other words, the revelator and the revelation are one and the same. The consultant, as well as the one who has called for help, are both the revelator and the revelation. In this way, it is clear that the Consciousness of the one who called and the Consciousness that is the revelator are inseparably One. *No so-called treatment needs to be given, nor are any truths sent out to the one who has called.* There is no one outside to whom a treatment can be sent. It is in this Oneness that immediate Perfection is perceived and manifested.

There is definite purpose fulfilled as every revelation of Truth that reveals — thus manifests — Itself. So, Beloved, you can perceive that even that which is called the negative has its purpose to fulfill. *It merely focuses the attention on, and as, the infinite All-Truth being revealed and manifested right here and now.* It is in this way that the Heaven that *is* this Earth is perceived, experienced, and evidenced.

Now let us speak of the third and last point of our clarification. As you know, there is a second segment of this continuous class. If there are certain statements herein that seem obscure, you may rest assured that these statements will be completely revealed and clarified in this second and last segment. This first is absolutely necessary as a preparation for the Truths revealed in the second. Furthermore, the second part of this work should not be read or studied until the first part has been studied and the reader has had an opportunity to contemplate the Truths revealed herein.

Beloved, I have made the foregoing statements here and now because we are going into the closing, all-important section of this book, and I do not wish to interrupt the continuity of these further revelations.

Chapter XXVI

Revelation, Identification, Manifestation

Any Fact, or Truth, is an eternal, infinite, complete *Certainty*. There is no temporary Fact, or Truth. There is no separate Fact, and there is no incomplete Fact. *Any Fact or Truth is a universal, eternal, constant Existent.* Any Fact precludes the possibility of an opposite of Its Truth. Every Fact is an absolute Certainty. There can be no uncertain Fact, or Truth. Every Fact is an unqualified Truth. Every Fact is a complete Truth.

Revelation is a Fact, or Truth, revealed. Revelation is a disclosure of an existing Fact, or Truth. A Fact is revealed when full comprehension of this Fact supersedes any supposed misapprehension about this Fact. When misunderstanding of the Fact is completely transcended, revelation discloses the Fact, or Truth, that does exist. In short, understanding of any Truth, or Fact, dissolves any apparent misunderstanding of this Fact.

Once a Fact, or Truth, is known — understood — there is no knowledge of, or concern for, any supposed opposite of this Fact, or Truth. Only that which exists can be revealed or disclosed. Any Fact, or Truth, is an eternal, constant, omnipresent Existent.

Thus, all revelation or disclosure has to be the existing Fact revealed.

God is the Revelator, or the Revealer. Man is the Revelation; thus, Man is the Revelator—God—revealed. The Revelator cannot be separate from or other than the Revelation. This is true because the Revelator can—and does—reveal *only* Himself or Itself. You see, God being All, there is nothing that God can reveal that is not God. Thus, God is the Substance of His own Self-revelation.

All revelation is Self-revelation. Only that which is true as God is true as Man, who is God's revelation of Itself. Thus, God revealing Itself is God being Self-revelation. It is in this same way that Man can only experience Self-revelation. Man can only reveal—disclose—to and as Himself that which Man truly *is*.

All revelation is Fact, or Truth, revealed. Let us perceive just what are some of the inseparable Truths that God reveals Itself, or Himself, to be. God is eternal, immutable Life, Consciousness, Intelligence, Love. God revealing Himself is eternal, immutable Life, Consciousness, Intelligence, Love. Man is God's revelation of Itself. So Man is eternal, immutable Life, Consciousness, Intelligence, Love. But God is also constant Perfection. God's revelation of Itself as Man is constant Perfection. In short, every Truth that God *is*, is revealed as Man. And the Fact that God is Self-revealed—or Self-revelation—is also the Fact that Man is Self-revealed, or Self-revelation.

171

This, Beloved, is why we know that all revelation has to be Self-revelation. Thus, you can perceive why it is impossible for anyone to reveal your Self to your Self, as your Self.

All that Man can reveal to Himself is just what Man now and eternally *is*. Nothing can be revealed *to* or *as* Man that is not already a Fact existing as Man.

Beloved One, the two foregoing statements of the Absolute Truth are of tremendous significance and importance. It would be well for you to study and contemplate deeply these two statements.

You see, heretofore, we have been prone to consider revelation as something that God revealed *to* us. Some of us even imagined that God must reveal Itself through an intermediary called a teacher, leader, etc. More recently, we have recognized the Fact that God revealed Himself as our own Identity, Being, even Body. But now it is absolutely necessary that we see farther than ever. That which must be perceived is the fact that Man's only revelation has to be just what Man is, has always been, and will forever be, disclosed as the very Self-Consciousness that *is* Man.

There is no Man outside of, or other than, God being. There is no God being the Christ other than Man, or the Christ, being. And this forever Fact, or Truth, is the true and *only* revelation. You will recall that we have stated in previous writings that God being the Christ is Man and that Man being the Christ is God. God, Christ, and Man are One and the Same; and this One is the basic Fact, Truth, that exists as all there is of Man. Furthermore, this basic Fact is all that can be revealed or disclosed as Self-revelation.

Now, it does appear that there are three aspects of Man's full and complete revelation and the manifestation of this Self-disclosure. These aspects are Revelation, Identification, and Manifestation. We have just discussed the first of these three aspects of Self-revelation. Let us now explore the second aspect of Man's Being, which is Identification.

We can know all the Truth there is to know and yet apparently be devoid of the evidence of our knowing. Oh, we've seen it happen again and again. We have questioned, "Why is it that I know this Truth so well, and yet it is not evident?" All of us seemed to experience, somewhat, this frustration in metaphysics. And some of us appear to have this experience even though we have gone beyond metaphysics and are seeing from the standpoint of the Absolute. The question is, "Why should this seem to be the case?"

The answer is in the revelation of Identity, or Self-identification. We cannot be the infinite Identity that we are without also being the specific Identity that we are. Neither can we be the specific Identity that we are unless we are also the infinite Identity that we are. The universal Identity that we are is the

173

specific Identity that we experience being right here and now. It is the infinite, but specific, Identity that lives, acts, moves, and has his being right here as our daily experience. It is the infinite, being the specific Identity, that works, plays, maintains a home, a business, or a profession. It is the infinite Identity, being the specific Identity, that fulfills a definite purpose right here, even though that ful-fillment of purpose may *appear* to go on through so-called human activities. We cannot even walk across the room unless it is the infinite—but specific— Identity walking.

Let us not be deceived here. The specific activity, or experience—although it seems to be a human experience—*is not the experience of a born man. There is no born man that can experience anything.* Yet our so-called human activities and experiences do appear to go on in a material world and as the experience of a suppositional human being.

It is small wonder that we seem to be deceived by the appearance of a material world, with appar-ently born beings, bodies, and activities. It is true that even when we experience that which the world calls healing, it is manifested as something that cer-tainly appears to be a born, physical body. And if some business, home, or supply problem is solved through spiritual perception, it does appear that the change takes place in and as the supposedly human activities and experiences.

When visible Perfection supersedes *apparent* imperfection, it may seem that Spirit, Consciousness, manifests Itself as matter. Spirit—Consciousness—is never matter, and genuine spiritual experiences are never the experiences of supposedly born man. Nonetheless, there are experiences going on here and now as our specific experiences. There is fulfillment of purpose going on here and now as *our* specific—yet infinite—fulfillment of purpose. But you see, we look right at Consciousness, Spirit, in Form and imagine it to be solid, dense, sometimes imperfect, and temporary. Being specific has absolutely nothing to do with apparently being separate, dense, solid human beings or bodies.

We know full well that we are infinite, inseparable, omnipresent Being. But we also know that there is someone here and that this someone is an Identity. We know that there is activity, moving, breathing, laughing, speaking, etc., right here and now. If we were not a specific as well as an infinite Identity, we would not be aware of acting, moving, being right here. Who or what is it that is moving, acting, breathing, experiencing right here? It is the infinite Identity that we are, focalized as the specific Identity that we are. What is it that is alive here? It is the boundless, universal Life that we are living here and now.

Right here is where the importance of the words *I AM* become so very powerful and significant. I AM is the infinite Identity. I AM is the infinite Identity

175

that I am, being the specific Identity that I am. I AM is the specific Identity being the infinite Identity that I am.

Oh, beloved One, there is infinite power in this perception. But there is also tremendous humility. *Without humility, there could be no power.* Humility and Love are identical. Without humility, there could be no Love. Without Love, there could be no humility. Power that is devoid of the Love that is humility would indeed be a terrible thing to even consider.

> The infinite Power of this perception is the Allness, the Entirety, the Totality that governs Itself as this entire Universe, and this Power is omnipresent Omnipotence.

Isn't it wonderful—and awesome—that we can say, *"I am that Power, and that Power is the Identity that I am?"* But just let us try to use this Power for some little selfish, so-called purpose of our own, and we will quickly discover that we are seemingly completely helpless and powerless. No, this is not a power that can be used. It is simply a Power of being what we *are* and *All that we are.* And we are completely aware that the very same omnipresent I AM that we are is the very same indivisible, omnipresent Omnipotence that exists as *every* Identity.

It is indeed necessary to be both specific and infinite in our "seeing," or perception. Only in this way can we be certain that the full Presence and Power that is our infinite Identity will be manifested as our daily living and experience. It is in this perception that our Substance in Form called Body manifests Itself to be Absolute Perfection. It is in this way that the illusion called age is dissipated. It is in this way that every seeming problem common to so-called born man is completely transcended. Thus, we see and experience the kingdom of God *right here, in and as our daily affairs.* We discover that we are indeed in the temple of God and that *we are the temple itself.* We really know the meaning and significance of the statement, "Earth is Heaven misunderstood, misperceived, and misinterpreted."

Beloved, here we stand. We can do no other.

Chapter XXVII

Manifestation

Now that we have discussed the first two aspects of our revelation, let us proceed to investigate the third aspect of complete Being, which is *manifestation*. What is the use in all our "seeing" if it isn't manifested in and as our daily experience and as our entire Being? This means that our illumined perception must be also evidenced as our Body. *Without Body, there would be no Completeness; thus, there could be no complete fulfillment of purpose manifested or evidenced.*

Yes, even that glorious One called Jesus found it necessary to reveal, identify, and manifest himself as the Completeness which was visible Substance in Form—or Body. The Body was, and is, necessary to Jesus' complete fulfillment of purpose, and his stupendous fulfillment of purpose continues to go on and will continue to go on, ad infinitum. But if Jesus had been bodiless, could his purpose have been—and continue to be—so beautifully fulfilled? No! Since visible Body was necessary in order that Jesus' purpose be completely fulfilled, it is certainly necessary for us to be visibly manifested as Form and Activity called Body.

Of course, we must always be aware of the fact that *all fulfillment of purpose is — and has to be — the Infinite All, God, completely, perfectly, fulfilling His purpose in being All*. This is true, even though the infinite purpose is fulfilled as the specific purpose, even as the Infinite All, or Identity, manifests Itself as the specific Identity. Lest we seem to be repetitious, we will not continue any further with this subject. But it will be helpful to contemplate deeply in this vein and experience your own ever greater revelations,

Infinite Perfection fulfills Its purpose by being infinitely and specifically perfect. Therefore, infinite Perfection manifests Itself as the perfect Substance, Form, and Activity that It constantly, eternally is. In order that our purpose in being be completely and perfectly fulfilled, the *manifestation* of Perfection must be experienced in, and as, every iota of our Being. It is absolutely necessary that perfect Substance as perfect Form and Activity be evidenced *as the Body*.

Absolute Perfection does manifest Itself as what It is. Thus, Perfection manifests Itself as perfect, immutable Body. Perfect Body is necessary to complete, perfect fulfillment of purpose, and this perfect Body must be visible and experienceable, even as Jesus' perfect Body was — and is — visibly evidenced. Actually, there is no Body in existence that is not Perfection *being* that specific Body. This, Beloved, is why every Body is, and remains, absolutely perfect.

Now, let us perceive, thus experience, the manifestation of this perfect Body.

The ultimate Absolute Perfection is the immediate, certain fact that *Absolute Perfection is*. Perfection, far beyond any so-called human imagination, is an absolute, certain Fact, right here and now. Just imagine, if you wish, what would be the most glorious experience of being you could know and then realize that this perfect experience is present as an absolute, certain Fact right now.

Yes, a more perfect Body than it is possible to imagine is a certain Fact as this Body, right here and now. Supply, far beyond anything we could imagine, is a certain Fact of, and as, our Existence right here and now. Beauty that is indescribable is our very Substance, our Form, our only living experience right here and now.

Oh, Beloved, don't you see, it is all here; it is all now. It is all a manifested Fact right *here* and *now*. The Fact *is* the Manifestation. The Manifestation *is* the Fact. *You are the Fact, and you are the evidence of being the Fact.* How, then, can you possibly be unmanifested? There is no unmanifested Fact. Admit the Fact. Admit the Manifestation *as* the Fact.

> Admit that you are the Fact that is the Manifestation and that you are the Manifestation that is the Fact. Further you cannot go. Just stand right here.

Every Absolute Truth that God *is*, is revealed in our beloved Bible. All that is necessary is that we perceive the Truths behind and beyond the words and the lines. Perhaps one of the most significant statements of Substance in Form revealed in our Bible is the following quotation:

> For in him dwelleth all the fullness of the Godhead bodily. And ye are complete in him, which is the head of all principality and power (Col. 2:9-10).

Of course, Paul was speaking of the Christ, and here he clearly reveals the necessity for every one of *us* to perceive that He is the infinite Christ Itself. And the infinite Christ is God, for there is none else for Christ to be.

According to so-called born man's opinion, his intelligence is assumed to be centered in the brain or head. This assumption is, of course, ridiculous. But the "fullness of the Godhead" is a statement of tremendous significance. This word *fullness* really means Completeness, Allness, Onliness. It denotes boundless, universal Mind—all Intelligence—all Knowledge. It means that the infinite Christ-Man, God-being, is this complete All-Knowledge—Intelligence. It signifies that the Christ-Mind (Intelligence) is the full and complete knowledge of *every Truth* and that this infinite Christ-Intelligence is *complete* as the knowledge of the sum total of all Truth. It is not surprising that Jesus clearly said, "I am the Truth." And this blessed One knew what he was talking about. But Jesus also knew that being the "fullness of the Godhead" meant being all Knowledge, all Absolute Truth Itself.

Let us now perceive the significance of the word *bodily* at the close of this statement. The "fullness of the Godhead bodily" really means the complete Mind (Intelligence), all Knowledge—in Form. It is no mere happenstance that the word *bodily* appears in this statement. As has been so often stated, all Substance exists in and as Form, and *Form means Body*. Whether we speak of the Form—Body—of a tree, a bird, a star, a planet, or whatever, we are speaking of Substance in *Form*. But the Body, or the Christ-Body, is the Completeness—that full, complete Self-Knowledge—which is God, being the Christ, or Man.

Paul's statement "And ye are complete in him" really means that *we* are complete *as* the fullness, the Allness, that *is* all Knowledge, all Truth—all that is true—and all Being. But Paul has also said that this Completeness that we are exists "bodily," or as the Body. This is a wonderful statement. It really means that this Body, right here and now, consists of the full, complete Mind — all-knowing Intelligence — which is God. Beloved, *this* Body that lives, moves, and breathes right here and now *is* full, complete Intelligence Itself. It is conscious; thus, It is Consciousness. It is alive; thus, It is Life. It is perfect, harmonious; thus, It is Love Itself.

Omnipotence is Absolute Truth; It is a certain, existing Fact. Therefore, the very Substance that is this Body is *the power to manifest Itself as just what It is.* (There will be much more on this subject in the final segment of the class.) This book would not be complete without this one important statement. Let it be repeated:

> This Body right here and now is the power to manifest Itself as just what It is.

This, Beloved, is "the fullness of the Godhead bodily."

And now in joy, in absolute certainty, and in awesome humility, we can contemplate in the following way, or in any way that is revealed as our Consciousness:

> I am the Revelation and the Revelator. I am the Identity and the Identifier. I am the Manifestation and the Manifestor, for I AM THAT I AM. I am the living, conscious, loving, intelligent evidence of the Fact that *God is All, All is God.*

> I am the evidence of things apparently unseen. I am the conscious evidence of the seemingly unseen Consciousness — God. I am the intelligent evidence of the seemingly unseen Mind — God. I am the loving evidence of the seemingly indivisible Love — God. I am the living evidence of the apparently unseen Life — God. I am the perfect evidence of the seemingly unseen Perfection — God. I am the immutable evidence of the apparently unseen Immutability — God. I am the constant evidence of the seemingly unseen Constancy — God. I am the eternal evidence of the apparently unseen Eternality — God.

I am the beautiful evidence of the apparently indivisible Beauty—God. I am the absolute evidence of the assumed unseen Absolute Truth—God. I am the total evidence of the supposedly unseen Whole, Entirety, Completeness, Totality—God. I am the omniactive evidence of the apparently invisible Omniaction—God. I am the rhythmic, perfect activity of all the rhythmic tempos which comprise Omniaction, or God in action.

I am the Presence of the Omnipresence which is God. All God is am I, for there is none other for me to be.

All of this am I, for I AM THAT I AM.

About the Author

During early childhood, Marie S. Watts began questioning: "Why am I? What am I? Where is God? What is God?"

After experiencing her first illumination at seven years of age, her hunger for the answers to these questions became intensified. Although she became a concert pianist, her search for the answers continued, leading her to study all religions, including those of the East.

Finally, ill and unsatisfied, she gave up her profession of music, discarded all books of ancient and modern religions, kept only the Bible, and went into virtual seclusion from the world for some eight years. It was out of the revelations and illuminations she experienced during those years, revelations that were sometimes the very opposite of what she had hitherto believed, that her own healing was realized.

During all the previous years, she had been active in helping others. After 1957, she devoted herself exclusively to the continuance of this healing work and to lecturing and teaching. Revelations continually came to her, and these have been set forth in this book.

To all seekers for Truth, for God, for an understanding of their own true Being, the words in her writings will speak to your soul.

71679335R00113

Made in the USA
Columbia, SC
06 June 2017